CREATIVE CHILDREN'S SPACES

Ashlyn Gibson

With photography by
Ben Robertson

CREATIVE CHILDREN'S SPACES

Fresh and imaginative ideas for modern family homes

rps

RYLAND PETERS & SMALL
LONDON • NEW YORK

This book is for my sister Caryl — chief den-builder and childhood playmate.

First published in 2015 by
Ryland Peters & Small
20–21 Jockey's Fields
London WC1R 4BW
and
519 Broadway, 5th Floor
New York, NY 10012
www.rylandpeters.com

10 9 8 7 6 5 4 3 2 1

Text © Ashlyn Gibson 2015
Design and photographs
© Ryland Peters & Small 2015

ISBN: 978-1-84975-665-5

A CIP record for this book is available from the British Library.

Library of Congress CIP data has been applied for.

Printed and bound in China

Senior designer Toni Kay
Senior commissioning editor Annabel Morgan
Location research Jess Walton
Production David Hearn
Art director Leslie Harrington
Editorial director Julia Charles
Publisher Cindy Richards

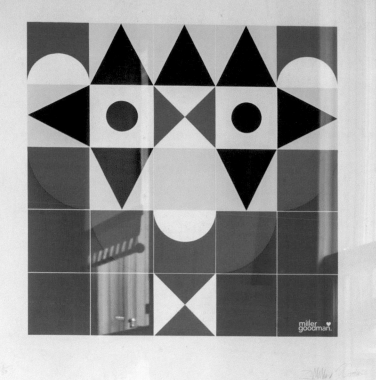

CONTENTS

INTRODUCTION

Children discover the world around them via their natural curiosity and hunger for knowledge. You may be faced with a hundred questions a day, but the more you engage with your children, the richer they will become. *Creative Children's Spaces* celebrates the many daily voyages of discovery that you can make at home with your child.

A creative family home has an abundance of inventive and resourceful ideas that encourage children's fertile imaginations. These essential ingredients for a stimulating childhood don't have to come with a big price tag. You can find a use in everyday household items for imaginative play, and discover the potential in recycling for art projects and den-making.

Creative Children's Spaces salutes communal spaces where the family can come together. Even a high chair pulled up to the kitchen table can be the launch pad for an inspiring childhood. In a successful family home, the smallest of spaces can provide boltholes and hideaways where your children can grow in independence. For older children, homework zones offer a place where they can to develop their concentration and start to organize their own lives.

Every home that I visited for this book was a revelatory example of an ongoing collaborative project. They all responded to the changing needs of the children who inhabited them. From a vibrant modernist home in London to a rustic cabin on the edge of a forest in Warsaw, Poland, each had its own spirit and soul. And at its centre was the creative energy of the children who live there.

OPPOSITE I like things to have a dual purpose at home. Houseplants not only inject colour and life into a nursery, but they also act as props for storytelling and imaginary play. I grew up surrounded by such a huge selection of houseplants that we used them as a jungle hideout. The parlour palm (*Chamaedorea elegans*) shown here is an easy houseplant to grow; it's fairly inexpensive and suited to indoor life.

ROOM TO GROW

ABOVE Invest in beautifully made wooden heirloom toys. This Ostheimer Noah's Ark is perfect for floor-based play and can be reinvented throughout childhood. It was my daughter Olive's most-loved toy and came from her granny. Each birthday and every Christmas, a new pair of animals was added to the menagerie and she grew up talking to the animals.

WITH SOME THOUGHT AND PLANNING, AN INSPIRING NURSERY CAN BE ADAPTED IN AN APPROPRIATE WAY AS YOUR CHILD REACHES DIFFERENT MILESTONES. ELEMENTS CAN BE ADDED, SUBTRACTED OR CHANGED SO THAT THE SPACE EVOLVES AS YOUR CHILD GROWS. DON'T BE DRAWN INTO THE COMMERCIAL WORLD OF GENDER STEREOTYPES – THEY HINDER THE IMAGINATION AND SUPPRESS INDIVIDUALITY. AS A STARTING POINT, CHOOSE A WALLPAPER THAT MAKES A BOLD DESIGN STATEMENT. IT'S MORE LIKELY TO KEEP YOUR CHILDREN ENCHANTED AND WILL STAND THE TEST OF TIME.

Nesting is a natural instinct that helps you to prepare for the arrival of your baby – it's an exciting time that will involve some reorganizing of your home. There are lots of nursery and baby products on offer, but think carefully before buying into the world of 'must-have' items. Stick to the basics, and you will probably find that you don't need much more.

Put your energy into making something original for the nursery. I spent some time in the Scottish Hebrides before my daughter Olive was born and made a talisman out of driftwood and shells. I carved the wishes that I had for her into the wood and tied it together with string. We still have it and it serves as a reminder of that special time.

A nursery should meet the changing needs of a growing child. There are many directions that you can take, but why not start your journey into parenthood with a bold statement? Black-and-white wallpaper will appeal to the monochromatic vision of a newborn. For older children, it will create a backdrop that they can colour in,

or one that can be "coloured" with their imagination. I haven't seen anything more exciting than The Wild by Bien Fait, a panoramic wallpaper inspired by Henri Rousseau. This larger-than-life illustration will take children on a journey through the jungle. As their awareness increases, they will notice more details, and these will keep their fascination alive.

It's impossible to foresee what your baby's sleep routine will be like, so trying to choose the right cot/crib is a daunting task. If you decide to co-sleep, a moses basket or a cot/crib may be outgrown before the cost of its purchase has been justified. A cot bed or convertible crib that becomes a toddler bed may be a more practical buy. Junior beds take up more space, so look for options that incorporate practical and space-saving storage.

A Boucherouite rug or rag rug on the floor is a modest but cosy start to kitting out a nursery. Large rugs add warmth and interest to a floor and are more versatile than fitted carpets.

LEFT As your children grow, adapt their spaces to suit their needs. Dressing-up clothes hung on the wall denote a place for playtime and imaginary games. A mirror ball connected to the electricity supply creates a magical effect that outshines any conventional mobile. From a source of fascination in early childhood, it will last into the teen years and beyond.

THIS PAGE **As children grow older, they accumulate more keepsakes. Here, old drawers turned into pinboards are ideal for displaying special treasures. Every bedroom should have a surface that children can decorate in their own way, and a wardrobe is a great base for an evolving collection of stickers. It will become a fun project where your children can express their own personalities.**

THIS PAGE AND OPPOSITE BELOW LEFT **Keeping on top of endless pieces of paper can be quite a challenge for adults and is even more difficult for children. A series of clipboards hung on a bedroom wall or in a study area keeps important items to hand and provides a fun and effective way of categorizing things.**

You can roll them back when you want to make room for messy play. Over time, and with the addition of a desk and task light, a snug play zone for a baby or toddler can easily evolve into a tranquil homework zone for a school-age child.

If you choose stackable boxes or modular units for storage, you can add to them when the need arises. Start with a toy box, add a dressing-up box during the toddler years, then follow the interests of your children. In Olive's case, we needed a box for her musical instruments. Create cosy reading corners in your living space as well as your child's room. Let children see that you too enjoy reading. Even before your child can read, pick up a book and talk about illustrations, play I-spy with pictures and help children to make up stories. Make books fun.

Houseplants bring a touch of nature into a child's room and naturally freshen the air, but make sure that you have chosen a non-toxic variety before placing a plant in a child's room – some popular houseplants, such as the peace lily, are poisonous to humans and pets. If you like the idea of plants but want to keep them away from little fingers, you could place them out of reach or create a hanging garden with 1970s-inspired macramé. A mini garden in a glass terrarium will be sure to capture an older child's imagination. Encourage them all the way by making up stories together about tiny folk in miniature lands.

ABOVE **The space beneath a pre-teen's bed can become a deep, dark void where things are apt to get lost or forgotten. My dad used draughtsman's chests as bed bases for my sister and me. The spacious drawers were perfect for storing large artworks and we loved them! Rather than investing in costly and cumbersome units, look for low cupboards, drawers or shelf units that can work as bed bases.**

COLOUR AND PATTERN

GROWING UP IN A COLOURFUL ENVIRONMENT CAN OPEN CHILDREN'S EYES TO A VIBRANT WORLD. A HOME ADORNED WITH PATTERN IS RICH IN INSPIRATION AND PROVIDES A STIMULATING BACKDROP FOR CREATIVE PLAY. GIVE YOUR CHILDREN THE CONFIDENCE TO EXPRESS THEMSELVES THROUGH COLOUR AND PATTERN.

ABOVE **Textile designer Mia-Louise has used colour to create a calm environment in her family home. Against a soft background she introduces splashes of more vibrant tones. Sons Huxi and Herbert have miniature remakes of French Tolix chairs that are destined to become family heirlooms. An art lover, she hangs paintings and posters that add blocks of colour and detail to the apartment.**

ABOVE RIGHT **If you live in a rental apartment, you will probably have neutral walls. You can still have fun with colour by hanging or propping up canvases. In stylist Sonja's rented home, a Friesian cow looms large over the kitchen table. The children find it amusing and it has become part of the furniture.**

A driving force behind opening my kids' store Olive Loves Alfie in 2005 was the desire to promote a new approach to colour. I found the obsession with the gender stereotypes of blue for boys and pink for girls limiting and predictable. The colour scheme of my childhood wasn't restricted, and I was determined that my daughter's wasn't going to be either. And so I set out to discover and promote a less-blinkered design aesthetic for children. A kaleidoscope of colour and pattern were staples in Olive's wardrobe and in our home decor.

Graphic designer Nina Nägel shares my view. "Colour and joyful prints have a positive impact – not just on children, but anyone. Colour makes one happy – who doesn't like seeing a rainbow?" In 2008 Nina relaunched her mum's vibrant 1970s designs for children. I applauded the arrival of new and revived brands that harked back to the cheery prints and bold palette of the 1970s, and parents flocked to my shop in pursuit of providing a colourful childhood.

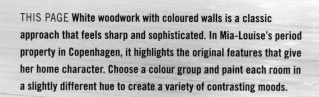

THIS PAGE White woodwork with coloured walls is a classic approach that feels sharp and sophisticated. In Mia-Louise's period property in Copenhagen, it highlights the original features that give her home character. Choose a colour group and paint each room in a slightly different hue to create a variety of contrasting moods.

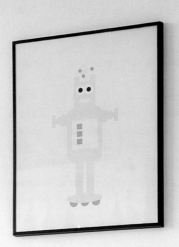

LEFT **Canvas storage sacks are easy to move from room to room and on warm sunny days Linda carries them out into the garden. The change of environment encourages the children to play with their toys in new and inventive ways. Choose a selection of baskets or sacks with varied patterns and designate each one to hold different things.**

RIGHT **A combination of natural wood, white gloss and sharp citrine turns a modular display into a colourful backdrop. A series of cubes sets the stage for a collection of cherished artefacts. Wooden birds designed by Kristian Vedel in 1959 perch beside children's pottery. An architect's model of this home reminds Thomas and Maiken of their vision for family living and their accomplished project.**

If you are going to redecorate your home, turn the decision-making process into a creative adventure with your children. It's relatively easy to pick up inexpensive ready-made canvases that can become permanent works of art. Investigate the huge spectrum of paint colours on offer nowadays and choose two or three sample pots each to try out at home. Don't try to sway your children towards your taste – instead, see what happens if you allow them to develop their own ideas. Childrenswear designer Aneta Czaplicka is fascinated to see how her five-year-old twins Kaya and Zuza express themselves through colour. "I listen to my children and I'm really surprised by the taste they have. They're not afraid to experiment, and that is beautiful." Be brave, let them play around with ideas and I guarantee your children will create some art worthy of hanging on the wall.

I am not a slavish follower of colour trends, but I am a great believer in surrounding yourself with colours that make you happy. If you like luxurious spaces and have a natural leaning towards one particular shade, try taking it to the darker end of the spectrum.

RIGHT **If you don't want to paint your walls, look around for other surfaces that you can decorate. The cupboard doors in the bedroom shared by Charlie and My have either been painted or covered with patterned wrapping paper. It has transformed their wall into a unique gigantic patchwork installation.**

LEFT AND BELOW LEFT **Yellow is optimistic and uplifting, and makes a refreshing choice for a boy's room. A platform bed can be useful in a shared bedroom. It helps to free up more floor space and creates a cosy den-like space underneath. In this room, decorating with vertical stripes gives an illusion of height that helps to make the concept work. Layer posters and prints over a striped wall to tell a story that will appeal to your children.**

OPPOSITE **If you want to achieve something unique in your home, introduce plenty of DIY decorating elements. Paper a wall with the C-60 Colour-Me wallpaper from Mini Moderns, which leaves the colour scheme to the imagination. It could be a project completed over a weekend, but there is something to be said for letting it evolve slowly. Start by choosing a few colours and see where they take you.**

THIS PICTURE **London-based fine artist Rob Ryan applies his paper cut work to many different media. This intricate wooden height chart makes a poetic statement and forms an enchanting addition to Nina's London family home.**

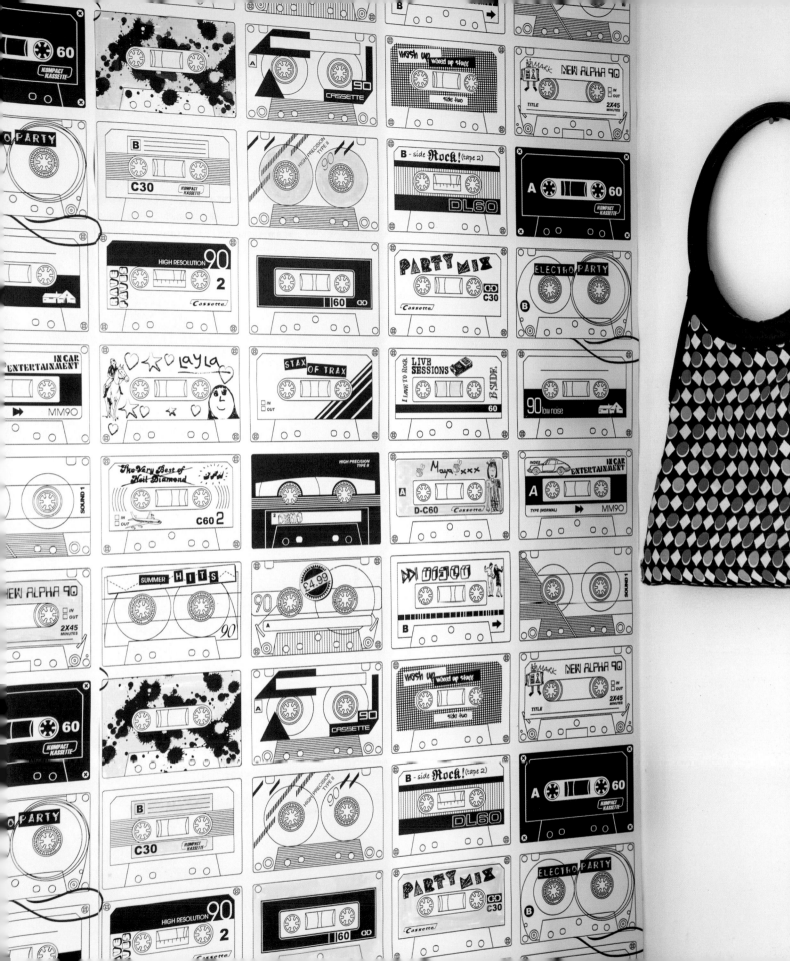

OPPOSITE **As children grow older, their tastes change. At 12, my daughter Olive is a self-confessed black addict so it felt timely to update her bedroom with a black wall. It creates a dark backdrop that is excitingly different and the perfect complement for pops of vibrant colour. The bespoke "Rebel" poster claims the space as well and truly hers.**

You might discover something rich and dramatic. If you feel more at home in a light and airy, ethereal space, explore softer, more subtle alternatives to optic white. Using the same colour on the ceilings, skirting/baseboards and doors will play down visual boundaries to create an illusion of space.

If you are a die-hard lover of clean white walls, there are plenty of other ways to enhance your home with colour and pattern. Add an injection of strong colour in the shape of accessories or furniture. A wallpapered feature wall is easy to update every few years and a bold print can immediately transform a child's room from a wintry ice kingdom to an exotic, leafy jungle.

As your children grow older, involve them in choosing paint or paper for their own room. Give them some decision-making power after all, taking ownership of your space is a rite of passage. When I was 14, I chose a huge tin of chocolate brown paint and decorated my bedroom myself. I am sure it wasn't to my mum's taste, but it was my room and she gave me free rein to choose whatever I wanted. I remember it as a milestone in my childhood.

ABOVE LEFT **Master embroiderer Laura Lees celebrates traditional craft with an anarchic rock-and-roll sensibility. She is part of a growing movement that is responsible for reviving old traditions so that they appeal to a new generation. Laura's Mexican Day of the Dead footstool has introduced Olive to the concept of customizing her own clothes with embroidered motifs.**

ABOVE CENTRE **Adding a mobile introduces the energy of movement to a quiet corner of a room. The Artecnica Themis Mobile in Maiken and Thomas's home adds a shot of fluorescent neon to their neutral living space.**

ABOVE RIGHT **Agata and Ian are devotees of the strong graphics and bold colours of Poland's rich heritage in poster design. They paid a visit to the Wilanów Poster Museum to choose a selection of colourful prints to hang in Bonnie's bedroom.**

THIS PAGE **There isn't anything contrived about the lively combination of colour and pattern in Jakob's bedroom, where monochrome prints mix quite happily with bright primary colours. A generous pile of cushions turns his bed into a cosy reading corner and provides an arsenal of ammunition for pillow fights with his brother.**

You are likely to find that your children have vivid imaginations and strong opinions about what they do and don't like. Mother of four Linda Hamrin Tait tries to take her children's ideas on board: "We always ask the children what colours they would like in their rooms. Oliver has always been a big fan of green and it has created a refreshing and vibrant space."

Lots of people tell me that they are afraid of strong colour, but painting a wall isn't an irreversible decision. Sample pots are there to experiment with and to make choosing the right shade easier. Children don't have the same set ideas as adults and, given the chance, may have radical but brilliant ideas. Photographer Emma Donnelly took inspiration from her ten-year-old son: "Inspired by the night sky, Monty was adamant that he wanted dark walls for his bedroom. We wanted to run with his idea, so we chose a colour that we thought was suitably dark but not too gothic." The result was a bedroom that reflects his personality and where he feels at home.

ABOVE **The Victorian fireplace in Nina's London home pays homage to her love of colour and print. She swapped a set of mugs from her design label ByGraziela for the big framed print. Letsswap.it is a progressive website where you can trade anything in return for art.**

LEFT **A piece of Ikea furniture has been given a clever makeover using hand-cut shapes from a sheet of sticky vinyl. Crafty mum Nina has transformed the chest of drawers into a unique statement piece of furniture.**

THIS PAGE **A sharp and graphic combination of optical white and vivid yellow walls creates a strong backdrop for a collection of retro-inspired prints. An unexpected parade of rustic wooden and beaded animals brings a poetic contrast and change of tempo.**

HOUSE OF CRAFT

THIS HOME IN POLAND'S CAPITAL CITY WARSAW IS AN HONEST AND LOVINGLY ASSEMBLED MIXTURE OF UPCYCLED MATERIALS, FLEA-MARKET FINDS AND HAULS FROM LOCAL SWAP MEETS. THREE GENERATIONS LIVE HERE TOGETHER, ALL SHARING A LOVE OF NATURE AND A PASSION FOR MAKING THINGS. KASIA'S MOTHER GRAŻYNA IS A CROCHET FANATIC WHO IS PASSIONATE ABOUT HANDING DOWN HER CRAFTING SKILLS TO HER FAMILY. THE KALEIDOSCOPIC COLOURS AND DESIGNS OF THEIR HOMEMADE TEEPEES, BLANKETS, WALL HANGINGS AND RUGS CREATES AN AUTHENTIC HOMESPUN VIBE THAT HARKS BACK TO THE 1970S.

Kasia and Robert Traczyk moved into their home five years ago with plans to make minor improvements. In reality, the 100-year-old house needed extensive renovations. They have carried out major works from the rooftop to the floorboards, but are very forgiving of flaws and embrace the imperfections that add character and personality to their home. The tranquil location on the edge of a forest is an idyllic spot to raise their two sons: Leon, aged six, and three-year-old Tymon. The neighbourhood is called Radość, which aptly means "joy" or "happiness" in Polish. Early 20th-century wooden shacks and summerhouses sit side by side with newer architect-designed residences on a patchwork of plots.

Kasia's childhood in a creative family has had a huge influence on her life. When she was seven she learned to use a sewing machine, and that early start blossomed into a working life as a designer/maker. With an abundance of creative energy, together she and her mother Grażyna run two handicraft businesses from home.

OPPOSITE **An abundance of handmade crochet items in Kasia and Robert's home ranges from miniature vegetables to cosy blankets. The round rug was crocheted by Kasia's mum Grażyna out of old T-shirts. It creates a floorcovering reminiscent of Missoni. The soft textures and muted colours of the family handiwork have turned their home into a well-crafted comfort zone.**

ABOVE **Kasia's label Radosna Fabryka was established to motivate children and parents to play creatively. Her range of soft shields and swords is central to Leon and Tymon's childhood games. The multi-coloured teepee in their playroom was made with a collection of new and old crochet pieces lovingly put together by their grandma.**

BELOW Hammock chairs are a fun addition to a family space. They take up very little room, but can provide hours of entertainment. A hammock can be anything from the base for wild and dizzy games to a quiet and relaxing spot to fall asleep in. Hung with a giant carabiner clip, they can be taken down if children are too young to play on their own. If you have a garden, find space to put a hammock outside in the summer.

RIGHT Things that have been handed down from generation to generation are interwoven with family stories that give them soul. Often too fragile to be used for their original purpose, family heirlooms can nonetheless be turned into pieces of art that you can draw enjoyment from every day. If you display them on the wall or find a different purpose for them, they will have more meaning than a new purchase.

Kasia has a collection of vintage and modern fabrics and trims that she draws upon for her designs. Inspiration often comes from found objects and there are always various projects on the go. Kasia spotted the potential in a collection of old wheels discarded from bicycles, scooters and trolleys, and these became the catalyst for a series of artworks that combine old and new in an inspired fashion. By covering the wheels with intricate lace tablecloths, she celebrates her grandmother's handiwork from the early 1900s.

Creative play and activities are fundamental to this family, as is being in touch with nature. Leon goes to an art class and comes home with inspired ideas for upcycling. The boys love painting with glue, covering it with glitter and attaching plastic eyes to make monsters. On family walks through the nearby woods, they collect birch sticks and feathers for craft projects. Although the children have a playroom upstairs, they are free to set up camp anywhere in the house or garden. They love imaginary games and are the best ambassadors for Kasia's range of tepees, dress-up crowns, soft swords and shields.

Kasia and Robert don't spurn modern technology or design, but are deeply attached to their collection of vintage furniture. Nothing pleases them more than finding something with a "Made In

Poland" label. Such pieces remind them of their childhood, when almost everything they owned was made close to home.

To make beds for the boys, Robert added industrial casters to upcycled wooden pallets. They can be moved around easily and the boys turn them into base camps for all sorts of games. Wooden crates, picked up from a local apple farmer, are put to use as storage for books and games. Everything that Robert makes for the boys is sturdy enough for them to climb and ride on.

This is a homespun environment where the emphasis is on community spirit. The laid-back rhythm of life in Radość allows everyone the space and time to explore their creative instincts.

What is your family motto?
Enjoy the moment when your children are small.

Describe your family in three words:
Happy shaggy crocodiles!

Kasia, what was your own childhood like?
It was very colourful. We were a very close family and it was always loud and crazy when we got together.

Did you have a particular vision for your own family?
I always dreamed of a large family. A big bunch of kids, maybe a dog and a small garden to plant some tomatoes and herbs.

Are you working on any new family craft projects?
A range of lampshades – I design them, Robert welds and paints them, and my mum makes the crochet elements.

Robert, what do you think makes for a happy childhood?
Freedom of play, and loving parents who get involved and treat their children as friends.

Leon, what is the best thing about living so close to the forest?
We have lots of visitors, including squirrels, hedgehogs, fat frogs, field mice, ducks, woodpeckers and lots of other birds.

Tymon, what is your favourite game?
Fighting with my mum's swords.

Grażyna, how does your life differ from those of your friends?
I have a passion for craft that keeps me busy and I get involved in many of Kasia's projects.

What do you enjoy making the most for your grandchildren?
Hats. They must have at least 30 each!

OPPOSITE **Kasia encourages the children to become involved in crafting and to share her passion for nature. The neighbouring forest provides the perfect place to forage for raw materials. Family crafting sessions around the dining-room table turn feathers and twigs into rustic wall hangings. Combined with handmade crochet, every piece is truly unique and is a work of family art.**

ABOVE RIGHT **The family's passion for the nearby forest is reflected in their use of different types of wood. The organic nature of wood has a quality that chimes with the rustic style of this home.**

RIGHT **Holding onto things from your childhood isn't always possible, but when it is, it gives your children a sense of family history. Leo and Tymon have inherited well-loved child-sized chairs that used to live in their grandparents' summerhouse.**

WONDER WALLS

USE YOUR WALLS TO PERSONALIZE YOUR SPACE.
COVER ONE WITH AN ASSEMBLAGE OF PERSONAL
ITEMS OR PHOTOGRAPHS TO ILLUSTRATE THE
UNIQUE IDENTITY OF YOUR FAMILY. TURN ANOTHER
WALL INTO A GIANT NOTICE BOARD THAT WILL HELP
TO KEEP FAMILY LIFE RUNNING SMOOTHLY.

Walls, like the pages of a book, can be utilized to tell a story about your family. All too often, I see empty expanses of wall that are crying out to be used. Quite aside from hanging beautiful wallpaper or making a colourful statement, there are limitless practical uses for walls that go beyond the purely decorative.

At home, we use one of the walls in our living room as a giant scrapbook where we display the things that we love. It is a snapshot of our lives at a particular point in time. Our favourite books are propped up on two rows of simple white Ikea picture ledges. Olive and I use picture hooks originally designed for wall mouldings to hang favourite pieces of jewellery. In the spaces in between, we stick postcards from friends, birthday cards, notes and tickets from holidays and festivals. It's a riot of colour and it makes us happy – it's as simple as that.

ABOVE **Three rows of simple shelving transform this wall into a library and gallery space. Mia-Louise incorporates child-orientated artwork alongside her own favourites to give her home in Copenhagen a family-friendly vibe. Little arrangements of toy animals add a child-like touch that make this a charming display.**

RIGHT **A fireplace provides space for a child's treasures. In Leo's room, a vibrant circus poster created by his grandma takes centre stage. Her designs are sold under the brand byGraziela. Playmobil characters are hidden in 3D letters, while postcards are displayed with washi tape.**

THIS PAGE **Rows of Ikea picture ledges provide a base for changing displays of your favourite things. Finding items that fit the constraints of a narrow ledge becomes a game. Miniature plant pots with small cacti are the perfect size. They bring a sense of the organic world into a vibrant display.**

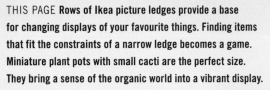

THIS PAGE Don't limit yourself to only decorating walls. Built-in cupboards often cover such large expanses of space that they lend themselves really well to vinyl decals. The wardrobe doors in Kamma's bedroom have become one of the room's most playful features.

DON'T
ENTER

Wallpaper can make a big impact and add instant mood and atmosphere to a room. Photographer Emma Donnelly wanted to add a wow factor to her seven-year-old daughter Agnes's room: "I chose a bold and graphic design that felt like a good compromise between girlish and modern." I can still remember the owl-print wallpaper that I had in my room when I was growing up. I used to invent stories about the characters before I went to sleep. If you hunt around, you can still buy original wallpaper from the 1950s, '60s and '70s that is unlikely to pop up anywhere else.

There is a vast range of wallpaper designs and styles to choose from. Some have been designed especially for children but will appeal to the whole family. Don't limit your choice just to children's designs. Many aimed at adults have a style and sensibility that will also capture a child's imagination and may well have a longer-lasting quality. The wallpaper that illustrator Silvia Pogoda chose for her own bedroom wall didn't need changing when it became 18-month-old Leo's nursery. "It is such a beautiful design that has universal appeal. It is a jewel and Leo loves it."

Floral designs and woodland scenes are dreamy and a good bet for a bedroom. Childrenswear designer Aneta Czaplicka looked for something with an intricate design that five-year-old twins Kaya and Zuza wouldn't tire of. "I imagined something beautiful and intricate. I picked wallpaper with butterflies, birds and flowers. My girls were fascinated when they saw it for the first time." Cleverly designed wallpapers can also evoke an interesting theme without being overly prescriptive. A print of cacti and cowboy hats is more inspiring than a "tell-it-all" wallpaper and leaves plenty of scope for a child's imagination. Striking geometric designs can be interpreted by different people in different ways. I loved talking to Olive about the

ABOVE RIGHT **These small neon triangle stickers give a graphic edge to Elin's room. The beauty of them is that you can keep on adding shapes and new colours. You could even carry on until you have created a Jackson Pollock-inspired sticker wall.**

RIGHT **Eccentric British design label Corby Tindersticks creates quirky toys that are imaginative and inventive. Made from felt, this world map is light enough to be stuck to a wall with washi tape. It can easily be lifted down for playtime.**

LEFT **A chalkboard wall encourages temporary works of art. Chalked designs can be changed whenever the whim takes you. Be spontaneous and try not to give your doodling too much thought. If you don't want to draw freestyle, look for templates that you can draw round to create repeat patterns. Here, a leaf from a houseplant makes the perfect template for a jungle-inspired design.**

ABOVE **A collection of sought-after vintage tin letters spells out the message of "LOVE". It is more than a declaration or style statement. Each letter also acts as a mini shelf where small fingers can balance tiny farmyard and jungle animals. Encourage your children to find little ledges and resting places for their favourite things. Humour and playful details give a home character.**

wallpaper in our old house. She saw an infinite number of shapes and her favourite colour changed almost every day. Textile designer Mia-Louise Mailund Smith wanted to use the walls in six-year-old Herbert and three-year-old Huxi's bedroom in a playful way: "I chose a bright yellow stripe wallpaper that reminded me of a circus tent." Larger-than-life panoramas can provide a magical backdrop for both sleep and play.

Smaller wall stickers make wall decoration a doddle. Graphic shapes, from raindrops to spots, give a room a modern edge. Children love stickers, so ask them to help or, better still, give them a wall of their own to decorate. Kids will bring a more spontaneous

THIS PAGE **A family home is incomplete without a gallery of family photos. There is something informal and spontaneous about a scattered arrangement. The random spacing of the pictures makes it easy to add new ones without being too precious or throwing the overall effect off balance.**

OPPOSITE **There is an incredible variety of wallpaper to choose from for children's spaces, enabling you to pick a design that reflects their personality. Children love the anarchic act of drawing on walls, but if your sense of freedom doesn't quite run that far, there are some great compromise solutions out there. This C-60 Colour-Me wallpaper from Mini Moderns is the perfect choice for hip young musos.**

and less rigid sensibility to design. And don't limit yourself to bedroom walls. Simple flat-pack wardrobes and drawers can become unique pieces of furniture when adorned with stickers.

Life-size wall vinyls can become a focal point for all sorts of imaginary games. From bold retro-inspired trees to elks, teepees and dreamcatchers, they can create a mood that encourages a spirit of creative adventure. Teacher Maiken Poulsen chose an unexpected vinyl for three-year-old Kamma's bedroom: "I wanted to move away from a stereotypical princess theme, so I chose a pirate ship. The plain white wardrobe doors made a great surface and it has turned that wall into a much more inspiring space".

A chalkboard-painted wall is ideal for an unused or overlooked space. It can become a family calendar as well as a place for spontaneous drawing sessions and scribbling notes. You could take it one step further and use magnetic chalkboard paint to create an even more versatile surface. Once you start looking at your walls in a new and inspired light, you will bring your home to life in original and unexpected ways.

ABOVE LEFT **Cork is a versatile and eco-friendly material. Available in thin tiles, it is inexpensive and fairly easy to cut, and as it's so lightweight it can be fixed to the wall with adhesive. You can buy pre-cut cork shapes ready to stick up, or make your own.**

ABOVE CENTRE **Whimsical details add a poetic touch to a white wall. Choose a design that isn't overly prescriptive to give you or your children artistic licence. These wall stickers from Mimi'lou give you scope for putting the stars wherever you like and could provide a starting point for a magical star-themed bedroom.**

ABOVE RIGHT **Illustrator Dan Golden's cartoons and illustrations have been made into a humorous range of wall vinyls. His Hole To Another Universe is an inspired fantasy portal to another world.**

LEFT Anything on a grand scale adds drama to a space. The large canvas in Malgosia and Przemek's living room makes a vibrant statement. The woman in the painting is lost in a world of music that resonates with one of the passions that is at the heart of this family.

OPPOSITE BELOW LEFT Malgosia adheres to the principle that if an item can be decorated, then why opt for something plain? She is committed to supporting Polish designers and collects porcelain mugs produced by Mamsam. They are used as a medium for cultural texts and carry the aesthetics of the Polish People's Republic and 1960s German design.

OPPOSITE ABOVE RIGHT Tiling the hall floor in the apartment provided an opportunity to introduce another layer of pattern. Decorative tiles hark back to the style of pre-war apartments in Warsaw, so they seemed like a natural choice. Malgosia likes the character of these monochrome cement tiles from Couleurs & Matierès. Being handmade, they have small imperfections that add to their artisan character.

HOUSE OF ILLUSTRATION

MALGOSIA AND PRZEMEK JAKUBOWSCY'S HOME IN AN OLD LIGHT-BULB FACTORY IN WARSAW IS ALIVE WITH ART, MOTIFS AND COLOUR. THE CHESTNUT TREES OUTSIDE THEIR LIVING-ROOM WINDOW CREATE A SEASONAL FRIEZE THAT VARIES FROM AN EMERALD FOREST IN SUMMER TO A SNOWY WINTER WONDERLAND. GROWING UP IN SUCH A WONDERFULLY EMBELLISHED HOME, NATALIA, AGED FIVE, AND JAN, AGED THREE AND A HALF, ARE NEVER SHORT OF INSPIRATION.

There isn't a hint of playing safe with neutral white walls in this home. Malgosia considers walls to be like blank pages in a storybook. She enjoys decorating them with her favourite wallpaper designs and vinyl decals to create a fantasy world in which her children thrive.

The wall treatments begin at the front door, which Malgosia painted with chalkboard paint to provide a blank canvas for the children to draw on. But before they could begin chalking, Natalia was playing with a magnet and made

RIGHT **Lighting plays a key part in creating the desired ambience in any room. This cheery oversized toadstool lamp casts a soft pink glow and is a great prop for games underneath the red tree vinyl decal shown opposite.**

BELOW **Children are experts at taking over spaces. They can see the potential for playing in places that we might overlook. Natalia and Jan turn the extra-long corridor that leads to their rooms into a bowling alley.**

a discovery that surprised everyone. Underneath layers of old paint, the door was actually metal. So now it is a magnetic notice board, and wherever they go the children avidly hunt for magnets to add to their collection. This entrance space is a happy mess where everything that is important to them finds a place – notices, invitations, children's drawings and photographs. The children haven't yet realized that the door can double as a chalkboard – no doubt that will be its next incarnation.

In the living room, a soft, chalky grey wall gives depth to the space and provides a subtle background for a lush tropical jungle canvas painted by Polish painter and installation artist Marcelina Wellmer. The vinyl stacked in an old Ricard box next to the record decks is a sure sign that this is a house where everyone enjoys music. Dancing isn't reserved for grown-ups or for parties but is part of daily life. When they want the children to have some downtime, Malgosia and Przemek take a trip down memory lane and play records from their own childhood collections of children's stories and songs.

They spend lots of time both as a family and with friends sitting around the breakfast bar that divides the kitchen from the main living space. Behind them the dappled light filtering though the treetops means the atmosphere changes with the seasons. Bird motifs add a burst of graphic verve to the kitchen and resonate with the sylvan setting. Row upon row of these have been printed onto Plexiglass, making a practical waterproof splashback that can be wiped down easily and quickly.

The original plan was to give the children a bedroom each, separated by a pair of sliding doors. Malgosia chose 1970s-style illustrations in bright

primary colours for Natalia's room. The adventurous spirit of the wallpaper, with its hot-air balloon motif, overturns conventional notions of what is suitable for a girl's bedroom, while a vinyl decal of a bold red tree becomes a prop for imaginary games. Jan's room, in contrast, embraces a softer palette including pops of pink. The unusual mix of two wallpaper designs – a dreamy cloud wallpaper and a fun and quirky robot print – differentiate between the play zone and the sleep zone.

However, a year or so ago Natalia and Jan spontaneously decided to rearrange the space themselves. It wasn't something the children could carry out without help, but they had a plan that

THIS PAGE **Wall stickers or decals are quick and easy to apply and offer a creative alternative to wallpaper. Some are permanent, but there are lots of designs that are removable. They can be used to great effect to create a mood or to define a space. If you adopt the same spirit as Malgosia, a wall sticker is just the starting point for an ongoing collage. She looks out for bird stickers to perch on the branches of this jolly red tree.**

Malgosia embraced. The children wanted to move the beds into one room so that they could sleep next to each other and jump from bed to bed. This has proved to be an arrangement that works well, giving them enough room for a teepee as well as freeing up space in the playroom for two desks. There is plenty of floor space for other activities too, and sitting opposite each other creates a fun and collaborative vibe, whether they are painting or singing.

The two rooms have built-in cupboards with the ingenious addition of a child-sized porthole in the door. The children turn them into dens at playtime, or hide away in them if they don't want to brush their teeth! When friends visit, the girls occupy one den, where they hide from the boys to share their secrets, while the boys set up camp in the other. Having ample storage for toys means they can tidy up easily and are left with a calm place in which to sleep.

FAMILY Q&A

What is your family motto?
It doesn't matter where, what matters is with whom.

Describe your family in three words:
Crazy, spontaneous, loud.

Przemek, what type of music do the children like the most?
They like many different genres of music, from classical and free jazz to weird electronica. Just like us! They also love listening to musical fairy tales on old vinyls that I listened to almost 40 years ago.

Does your family have a favourite song?
It is a song about a boar from the soundtrack to Mister Blot's Academy – a Polish–Russian children's fantasy movie from 1984, based on the novel by Jan Brzechwa.

Malgosia, do you have a favourite season?
We love every season. Personally, I love spring when everything is blooming and waking up to life. But I also like autumn in Poland, when it is still warm but leaves have

their beautiful colours. We love going to the woods at this time of the year.

How do you embrace the seasons with the children?
We enjoy traditional Polish crafts that I remember from my own childhood. In springtime we make flower bouquets; in autumn we make figures from chestnuts and we love rolling in the leaves.

Przemek, was nature a big part of your own childhood?
We both grew up in cities, but we love nature and travel to the seaside, the woods and the mountains. We spend lots of time with the children in our small house in the Masuria (the Polish "land of a thousand lakes").

Natalia, which wallpaper do you like most in your bedroom?
The robot wallpaper, because they are very friendly creatures who protect me and my brother from bad monsters.

Jan, do you have a favourite hiding place?
The little hideaways in our wardrobes.

Malgosia has treated the walls in this inspiring family home as giant canvases that are there to be embellished with colour and pattern. She is a great believer in feeding her children's visual imagination while they are young and at their most open and responsive to colour and sensation.

LEFT **Everywhere you look, the eye is caught by interesting wall details. Even a small gesture, in the right space, can create interest. A hedgehog wall vinyl scuttling along the skirting board/baseboard is the perfect companion when children are playing on the floor.**

OPPOSITE **A potent mix of patterns, from chevrons to clouds, creates a rich storytelling environment. Illustrations and prints provide the inspiration for children to make up their own stories. Malgosia encourages their imaginations by asking them to draw pictures based on their ideas. This is a family project that will culminate in them making their own storybook together.**

CLEVER STORAGE

EVERY HOME NEEDS STORAGE SPACE TO HOLD

THE FLOTSAM AND JETSAM OF FAMILY LIFE.

HAVING AN ORGANIZED HOME IS REALLY ABOUT

MAKING MORE TIME FOR THE FUN STUFF – GIVING

EVERYTHING ITS OWN PLACE MAXIMIZES YOUR

AVAILABLE SPACE FOR CREATIVE PLAY.

BELOW **Dorothee Becker's classic 1960s design, the Uten.Silo, is the ultimate wall organizer. Comprising a collection of containers, hooks and clips, this piece of iconic design is user-friendly and versatile. It houses an amalgamation of random things that represent modern family life – stray toys and a pair of novelty sunglasses sit next to an oilcan and a metre rule as though it's the most natural thing in the world. And in a family home, it is!**

RIGHT **Tiny things have a natural propensity to roll under furniture, never to be seen again. The lid of a cardboard box, pierced with holes, creates a display area for Olive's neon earrings.**

FAR RIGHT **I love to reinvent things and give them new uses. Picture ledges from Ikea are easy to embellish and customize. Inspired by the hooks on a Uten.Silo, we added picture hooks to display favourite necklaces.**

Successful storage is all about finding ways to get the most out of your living space. Being organized and methodical doesn't have to stifle fun and creativity. Instead, it gives you more time to focus on all the things you enjoy.

We all have belongings and they all need somewhere to live. I'm not a neat freak, but having a place for everything keeps the decks clear and makes tidying up quicker. In a busy family home, it's par for the course for things to go missing. Learning how to be organized feels like a lifetime's work, but I'm finally getting there and seem to be losing things less and less. The challenge lies in encouraging children to be tidy without being too precious.

My best advice is to keep things simple. If you adopt a "less is more" mindset and have regular clear-outs, it will help your cause. Don't be afraid to say no to the offer of hand-me-downs if you simply don't have space for them. And if birthdays and Christmasses bring a tidal wave of new toys and games, it can be helpful to adopt a policy of "one in, one out". But be careful what you throw away – I have friends who remember their favourite toys disappearing without their consent. Storing presents away and reintroducing them one by one when your children are ready for a new focus can also add to their enjoyment.

THIS PAGE **Be inventive with your storage ideas to create something that has meaning for your family. A series of brightly coloured woven baskets from a summer holiday will bring back happy memories and also function as portable storage. Simply hooked on the wall, these baskets full of sheet music can be carried off to music lessons.**

THIS PAGE **Storage works best when containers are of a manageable size. Opt for low-level units that children can access by themselves. As your children's needs change, the plastic-tub drawers lend themselves to a multitude of purposes, from building blocks to school books.**

ABOVE LEFT AND RIGHT **Sometimes the simplest ideas are the best. Heavy-duty paper sacks clearly labelled for different items provide hard-wearing storage. Casters make light work of moving storage boxes around. Portable collections of toys can be played with around the home and garden. The easier their things are to move, the more your children will get out of them.**

If, like me, you are a collector, you will face a different type of challenge. Rather than tempering your passion, find a way to celebrate it. A carefully curated display is a canny way to store your treasures while adding interest and personality to your home. This applies just as much to children, who can find enjoyment in arranging displays of their bounty.

Small spaces present the biggest challenge, but you just need to look in the right place for inspiration. Conjure up images of camper vans and narrowboats, where space is at a premium. These tiny spaces offer family-holiday environments that hinge on clever storage. A tight ship is a happy ship, so utilizing every square inch by way of clever built-in cupboards, fold-away tables and hooks on walls is the name of the game.

Efficient custom-built storage solutions use space wisely and suit the clean lines of modern homes. If you embark on a new build or addition to your home, don't overlook the opportunity to incorporate seamless storage. Teacher Maiken Poulsen and economist Thomas Høy Jepsen made storage a core element of

RIGHT **The Mexican Day of the Dead makes a great theme for a pre-teen room. Look for accessories that enhance the concept, but also add elements of storage. A skull-shaped cork notice board is handy for locker keys and notes. A shopping bag makes a practical alternative to a laundry basket – you can even try to insist that your children carry it to the washing machine themselves! Customize existing pieces of furniture with a set of spooky skull handles.**

OPPOSITE AND BELOW **I have a passion for old-fashioned drapers' cabinets. They have become fundamental to the way we organize our things at home. The handy-sized drawers, originally designed for display, make it easy to see what you have in store. My favourite piece is a rare find salvaged from a gentleman's outfitters. It has a myriad of drawers that make it the perfect storage unit for a family and all its needs: a first-aid kit, art materials or even fruits and vegetables.**

their architect-designed home: "Integral storage has a positive impact on our living environment. It makes it easier to have a clutter-free home." Take time to consider what is unique about the needs of your family and plan your storage spaces accordingly.

Challenging spaces can result in the most interesting ideas. Textile designer Mia-Louise Mailund Smith felt that her children's room wasn't as spacious as it could be, so she carved out some extra space for storage. "I incorporated secret compartments in each of the steps that leads up to Herbert's bed. He has designated different steps for each of his things. He knows where everything belongs, so it's easy for him to keep his space tidy."

THIS PAGE Knick-knacks can add character and personality to a child's room. Encourage them to enjoy what they have by designating a set of shelves for their treasured things. A cute shelving unit can become an improvised space for miniature arrangements that children can change every day.

ABOVE My favourite place to store Olive's collection of paints, pots of glitter and sew-on sequins is in her great-grandma Alice's wooden sewing box. Designed with lots of compartments, it lends itself perfectly to storing and sorting small things. We were lucky enough to inherit ours, but they are easy to pick up on eBay. If you track one down, turn it into your own art box. The uses are endless.

ABOVE RIGHT Space-saving and multi-functional ideas can be invaluable in any home. Stackable, heavy-duty storage boxes double up as stools. Turn them into magical boxes of tricks by decorating them with markers. Make them personal by naming what is inside them.

RIGHT I picked this box up on my travels years ago. Over time it has served many purposes, from housing my styling kit to acting as a tool box. These days it has been given a new lease of life as a box for the counters and dice used in board games.

During the day, Mia-Louise lifts the mattress off three-year-old Huxi's bed to reveal two deep cupboards where the boys keep their extensive Lego collection.

Perhaps a more inspired approach is to design your space so that it is adaptable. Creating a home where storage can change with the evolving needs of your family requires careful consideration. It's smart to opt for modular systems that can grow along with your family and your budget. Casters on storage boxes and shelving units give you flexibility and the potential to move things around within your space. Being highly versatile, movable pieces make it easy to develop your ideas.

If you live in an old house, I urge you to resist slicing up the space to create integrated storage. It may seem like a necessity, but there are other, more imaginative solutions. Build on the character and personality of your home by sourcing interesting pieces of furniture that can be given a new purpose. If you can accommodate them, freestanding pieces of furniture can provide storage with charm and originality.

Walls are often dead spaces, but they can provide ideal storage solutions. Wall-mounted shelving or cubes keep the floor area free and create a feeling of space. They also allow you to display the things that you love. Your own unique mix of treasures adds to your story and the narrative of your home.

My granddad stored his tools in orderly rows on a wooden pegboard on his garage wall. At my school, our science labs were

ABOVE LEFT Coats, bags and hats can dominate the entrance to any home. Hooks that are too generous become swamped or fall off the wall. Keep them neat, but ensure there are enough hooks for your needs. A good idea is to give everyone a hook in their favourite colour.

ABOVE CENTRE Don't reserve hooks for coats! Small off-cuts of birch branches make simple rustic hooks that are the perfect size for headphones and cables.

ABOVE RIGHT A bank of hooks adds character and function to a child's room. Hooks will have more longevity if the design isn't overly childish.

OPPOSITE Sonja and Eric had a chess table in their café in Amsterdam. Over a long period of time, pieces got lost. With a thrifty mentality, Sonja always holds on to things to find new purposes for them. When she wanted to create an eclectic mix of hooks, she transformed the leftover chess pieces.

kitted out with these too. I like the honesty and simplicity of traditional pegboards, but there are some modern upscale versions that work brilliantly as coat hooks or wall tidies. In our case, we need a home for our travel passes, bicycle clips, headphones, Olive's school locker key, a pass for her weekly circus class, her school timetable and the keys to my shop. A pegboard close to the front door is the perfect utilitarian answer to keeping tabs on your family survival kit.

OPPOSITE **Clever storage ideas in Thomas and Maiken's modernist family home keep their space relatively clutter free. Giving things a dual purpose helps the cause and brings extra meaning to pieces of furniture. A simple box seat lifts up to reveal storage that is perfect for a family collection of shoes.**

RIGHT AND BELOW LEFT **When Mia-Louise designed Huxi and Herbert's bedroom, she incorporated storage in as many places as possible. At playtime, Huxi's mattress, placed on the floor, becomes a crash mat for rough and tumble. With the hinged sides folded down, his bed opens up into a play zone containing two huge boxes full of Lego and dressing-up clothes. Herbert's raised platform bed allows extra play space on the floor.**

ABOVE **Children love the concept of hidden treasure and magic compartments. Take a leaf out of Mia-Louise's book and create exciting and secretive places for children to keep their favourite things. Adopt their way of thinking and try to come up with some original and inventive storage ideas.**

THIS PAGE **It's heart-warming to see a beautiful uber-stylish home that makes children's games as much a part of the decor as a collection of hip travel guides. There is an honesty and functionality about the open storage that is quite literally an integral part of the furniture.**

HOUSE OF CHANGE

JEANETTE AND RASMUS WESTERGAARD FRISK RUN AN ARCHITECTURAL PRACTICE THAT FOCUSES ON DEMOCRATIC URBAN DEVELOPMENT AND SUSTAINABLE DESIGN. THEIR OFFICE MOTTO IS "DON'T JUST DESIGN FOR THE PEOPLE, DESIGN WITH THE PEOPLE", AND THIS PHILOSOPHY IS REFLECTED IN THEIR FAMILY HOME, WHERE THEY LIVE WITH THEIR DAUGHTER MY, AGED SIX, AND FOUR-YEAR-OLD SON CHARLIE.

The couple's intention was to create a flexible family environment that would fulfil their changing needs. Working with sustainable materials such as birch veneer, the couple have developed affordable, understated modular storage that embodies their design philosophy.

One half of their apartment in Copenhagen is devoted to an open-plan living space, while the bedrooms and bathroom occupy the other half. In the living area, white surfaces combine with natural plaster walls to create a feeling of calm tranquillity.

ABOVE **Celebrate the everyday things with a functional display of tableware. A collection of Japanese blue-and-white ware is more intriguing than a traditional tea set for children. Bowls of all sizes and shapes make teatime fun and are perfect for children's parties.**

RIGHT **Picture ledges from Ikea have become a staple of the contemporary family home, offering a neat place to display books and pictures. The black finish and the simplicity of the design echo the Japanese minimalist style of this home. The combination of children's storybooks and design books is a true reflection of the family.**

BELOW The large wall unit that Jeanette and Rasmus designed to incorporate Charlie's and My's beds makes use of every square inch of space. The cupboards and spaces for plywood storage boxes are integral to its design. The child-sized wardrobes are an inspired idea to encourage the children to start learning about being in charge of their own clothes and toys. Their own areas are identified with their names using the alphabet from Design Letters.

RIGHT The necessary tidying up and packing away of toys should be an integral part of children's play. It can become an enjoyable game when it entails parking wheelie boxes in their designated spaces.

FAR RIGHT Colour coding cupboard doors is a smart way to organize things for young children, helping them to learn their colours and to remember where things belong. It also inspires guessing games: "What's behind the green door?"

An orderly run of modular seating in the living area doubles up as practical storage. Colour, imagery and graphic design are introduced via their collection of books on art, design and travel, which sits on narrow picture ledges that run the length of the room.

There is a very simple nod to nature in this home. In the living room, for example, the only decoration is a delicate ginkgo tree mobile that celebrates their love of Japanese style.

The children's room demonstrates the Frisks' mastery of interior design. Originally one wall was lined with plain grey cupboards, which provided ample storage space, and the children slept in classic Danish Juno beds designed to change from a cot/crib to an infant bed. When they were outgrown, Jeanette and Rasmus worked on a solution to incorporate new beds. They moved the middle row of cupboards to their own room, and designed twin beds that slotted deftly into the remaining space. The cupboards have now become a framework for vibrant colour and pattern, with the doors either papered with sheets of giftwrap or painted in bright, solid colours.

The floating design of the children's beds encourages a multitude of imaginary games. My and Charlie can turn their beds into dens by hanging blankets from the cupboards above, and the resulting

THIS PAGE **All of the furniture in this home has been designed by Jeanette and Rasmus. The play kitchen is based on the same principle as their furniture. Built on casters, it can be moved from room to room. They haven't down-scaled things, but have adopted an approach of using a full-size tap/faucet and handles to give it more life-like appeal.**

LEFT **Children don't need an excess of kitchen toys when they can plunder your own utensils. With the obvious exception of sharp items, it's fun to combine your day-to-day things with their own miniature versions – and it reduces the need for additional storage space.**

RIGHT **This modular family of hooks, designed by Lars Tornøe, has been attached to the wall at different heights. Having hooks within easy reach encourages the children to hang up their own coats and hats, and when "The Dots" are unused, they form an interesting pattern on the wall.**

tent-like spaces are a favourite place for the children to sleep. Charlie likes to imagine that his bed is an aeroplane – no doubt this has fuelled his dream to be a pilot when he grows up.

The beds have functioned well, but they are now reaching the end of their life span. Jeanette and Rasmus have an innovative approach to using their space, so they aren't too concerned about the children having to share a room as they grow older. They have already come up with a new concept for a multi-wall system that will incorporate bunk beds with sliding doors and storage. The children can look forward to privacy and cosiness as well as a space that meets their needs.

On the other side of the bedroom, a wall-mounted notice board and desk system floats above the floor. It gives the children a space each for model-making and painting. Fabricated from birch veneer, it has a smooth brown coating that makes it easy for the children to tape drawings to it and to peel them off again.

This fusion of minimalist Nordic and Japanese style has created a simple, elegant aesthetic that celebrates the functionality of this home. With one eye on design and one on the changing needs of the children, Jeanette and Rasmus have made evolution and change the guiding principles of their home.

FAMILY Q&A

What is your family motto?
Life is a game, play it.

Describe your family in three words:
Humour, unity and diversity.

Jeanette, what is the key for a creative childhood?
Giving our children colour and flexible space. Living in a space that they can inhabit and change helps them to grow up with confidence. The experience of taking part in and shaping their surroundings is a foundation for life.

Do you have any storage advice?
Make it a part of everyday furniture, including beds, sofas and tables. That ensures you optimize your space and functionality.

Rasmus, what are the benefits of great storage solutions?
It stimulates the kids' creativity and contributes to a flexible and multiple use of space.

Do you feel it is important to introduce an element of nature into family homes?
It is a very important thing for us. Merging nature with the city is a big element in our urban design work.

Charlie, what do you like best about your bedroom?
My aeroplanes and my bed.

And what games do you like to play?
I like to play with my aeroplanes and to build dens.

My, what do you like doing in your bedroom?
Sitting at the desk and drawing, then sticking up my drawings.

Which is your favourite room to play in?
My bedroom!

DISPLAYING ART

CELEBRATE YOUR CHILDREN'S CREATIVITY WITH DISPLAYS OF THEIR PAINTINGS AND DRAWINGS. A HOME DECORATED WITH CHILDREN'S ART IS A CREATIVE HAVEN THAT ENCOURAGES LITTLE ARTISTS. WHETHER YOU HAVE A SIMPLE OR ELABORATE DISPLAY, IT WILL BREATHE INDIVIDUALITY INTO YOUR HOME.

LEFT **Now that my daughter is older, I can really appreciate that there is a fleeting moment before children become self-conscious about their drawings. The more you encourage them and the more you display their work, the longer they will hold on to their confidence. Celebrate their creativity with a patchwork of drawings attached to the wall with patterned washi tape.**

BELOW **Find a space in your home where you can display children's art at their own eye level, as this allows them to enjoy looking at their work too. A long sheet of paper stuck to a wall at just the right height acts as a makeshift easel where children will stand up to draw.**

When we were children, my sister and I loved to make and create. Our art was as much a part of the interior of our home as paintings picked up from antiques markets and my mum's 1970s handicraft art. It was a homespun environment that had a unique identity and a heartbeat unlike any other.

My sister and I each had a giant hessian-covered notice board where we could pin up our art. We loved the freedom of expression that we were given, and it encouraged us to keep on creating. It's easy to make a gallery of your children's work – there are endless ways to display art, from a formal arrangement to the more spontaneous showcase. Look around your home for empty spaces that you can put to good use.

A small area of wall can be transformed into an enchanting gallery of miniature drawings. If you have more wall space, devote an entire stretch to children's paintings or framed pictures. Journalist Ewa Solarz acknowledges her children's creativity by devoting a wall to their art in her living space.

OPPOSITE **If you give them the right framework, children can create their own display. With this clip system, commonly used in restaurants, you don't need tape or tacks. It's a great example of taking something industrial and giving it a child-friendly function.**

THIS PAGE **Vibrant colours contrast with a black background to create a dramatic display of children's art. Search for interesting colours outside the everyday palette. Djeco is my go-to brand for non-toxic, vivid art materials, and here coloured paper turns children's cutouts into striking silhouettes. Give your children the freedom to add their favourite pictures or collectors' cards. And remember to take photographs to chart the way their display grows through their childhood.**

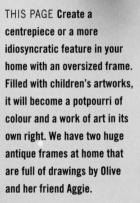

THIS PAGE **Create a centrepiece or a more idiosyncratic feature in your home with an oversized frame. Filled with children's artworks, it will become a potpourri of colour and a work of art in its own right. We have two huge antique frames at home that are full of drawings by Olive and her friend Aggie.**

THIS PAGE **Sonja de Groot's** home is full of intriguing displays where plants, antiques and children's art mingle together, and this old-fashioned glass-fronted cabinet packed with curiosities reflects her taste. Pick up something similar from a second-hand store and create your own wall-mounted display.

ABOVE Washi tape has become a must-have item in a creative family's tool kit. Sonja uses a sink plunger as an ingenious way of storing a tower of multi-coloured tapes ready to stick up her children's drawings.

LEFT Oliver and Astrid enjoy sitting at the kitchen table in their English seaside home. As soon as they have finished their drawings, they can display them on the wall behind them. A simple magnetic strip is the quickest fix. Each of the children has a white ceramic frame that gives a more celebratory effect.

"We put the children's art in frames. Jasiek (aged 12) and Marianna (9) are really proud of their creativity and so are we. It's important to celebrate their achievements."

A wall with a collection of family photographs interspersed with children's drawings or poems from significant moments tells a story that is unique to your family. Handprints, rudimentary attempts at spelling and notes that your children have written all deserve to be given a place in your family history. I see so many homes with shop-bought typographic posters that look great but leave me a little bit cold. I can't help feeling that children could produce something much more distinctive. Coming up with your own family motto is an interesting exercise. Not only is it an enlightening process, but once you have a motto, it can be the keynote for a handmade poster. When your children are older, you can step it up a gear and come up with a family manifesto that can be proclaimed on a handmade poster or canvas. Children's art is priceless, and

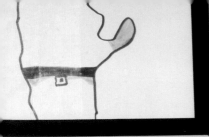

THIS PAGE **Ewa and Milosz put a happy emphasis on their children's art. A wall of budget picture frames is simple yet heartfelt. The matching nature of the frames gives the wall a uniform touch that suits their modern, minimalist home.**

the freedom and vibrancy of colour that is often found in their work will stand up against graphic-inspired art and bring a space to life.

There are many effective ways to showcase children's creativity. Try attaching a washing line to a wall in a hall – pegged with colourful art, it will lead you into the family home. Interior designer Sonja de Groot encourages her children to use their walls: "Sam and Lieve find spaces that become galleries of their work. They stick their pictures up with washi tape so it's easy to take down again."

For something more permanent, a hotchpotch of frames collected over time from charity shops/thrift stores will add a quirky twist to a display. If you prefer things to have an order, batch-buy half a dozen identical frames to start a gallery wall. Mother of four Linda Hamrin Tait sees the benefits in displaying her children's art: "It's not how much of their art that we show, but the effort they feel we put into displaying it. We bought them each a picture frame with the idea of changing the picture on display regularly."

OPPOSITE **Children can be prolific and, given the chance, would happily use an entire stack of paper in one session. Painting or drawing on a ready-made canvas creates a different mood altogether. The children will be proud of their results and a colourful canvas will look great on your wall. It will also make a touching present for grandparents.**

BELOW **Don't restrict children to making art with the usual materials. Give them interesting spaces to fill with their creativity. Olive uses an old drawer, upcycled with blackboard paint, as a chalkboard. There is a ledge to keep the chalk and it even catches the chalk dust too.**

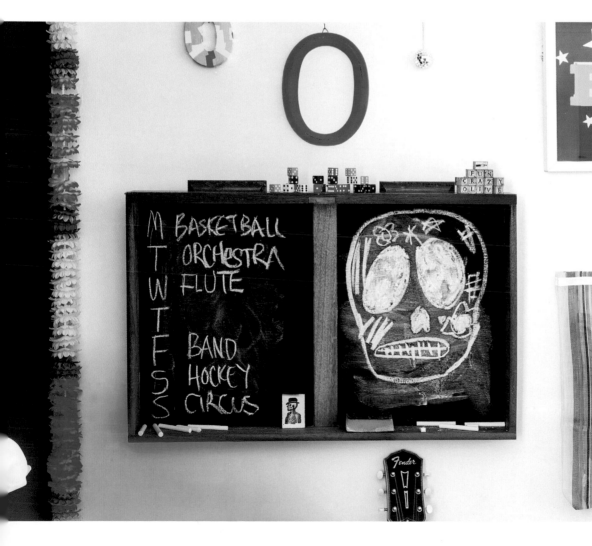

HOUSE OF CULTURE

OVER A PERIOD OF 15 MONTHS, FRAN FORCOLINI AND BARRY MENMUIR POURED THEIR IDEAS INTO A 1960S BUNGALOW ON LONDON'S DULWICH ESTATE. BARRY CARRIED OUT MUCH OF THE WORK HIMSELF AND MANAGED THE PROJECT, WHICH TRANSFORMED A RETIREMENT HOME INTO A CREATIVE FAMILY ENVIRONMENT. IT COMES AS NO SURPRISE THAT DAUGHTERS ANOUK, AGED SIX, AND RAY, THREE, BOTH HAVE AN ARTISTIC STREAK. THEIR PAINTINGS AND DRAWINGS POP UP ALL AROUND THE HOUSE IN MINI INSTALLATIONS AND ON GIANT NOTICE BOARDS.

LEFT A wall lined with open shelving is home to Fran and Barry's eclectic collection of taxidermy, ceramics and a set of Eames wooden figures. Fran's eye for striking colour and African craft contrasts with the polished concrete floor to create an environment that is rich in cultural reference.

LEFT Playing family games presents a real opportunity to spend downtime with your children. Games introduce children to colours, words and numbers. House of Cards, the construction game created by Charles and Ray Eames in the 1950s, is a family favourite here.

RIGHT **It's important to get children into the habit of recycling and reusing things where they can. Fran keeps a stack of empty egg cartons to use as paint palettes.**

Fran and Barry have an impressive collection of fine mid-century furniture, but in their bright, cheerful home this plays second fiddle to the creative efforts of their children. An open-plan kitchen and spacious dining room are at the heart of this home. Fran's Italian love of hospitality and cooking shines through in the kitchen, and the space transforms easily from a warm and welcoming culinary domain into an art room for the girls.

BELOW LEFT **A well-stacked art trolley gives the girls an array of materials to use. Children love sorting things into colours, sizes and shapes. Encourage them to respect their own materials and turn tidying up into part of the creative process.**

THIS PAGE **It's a matter of course that almost every day Fran turns the dining room into an art studio for the girls. A Tripp Trapp chair gives Ray a solid base to stand on to look over her work.**

OPPOSITE **A series of family portraits painted by Anouk is displayed on painted mannequin hands salvaged from Fran's boutique and screwed into the wall. Spontaneous and naive, children's art can be incredibly engaging. Ask your children to paint a new series every year (write the date of the painting on the back of the artwork) and add them to a growing family collection. It will be fascinating for them (and you) to look back on when they are older.**

In between meals, the girls trundle their art station into the dining room from the bedroom. Fran keeps the vintage trolley stacked with an abundance of new and recycled materials that can't fail to excite and inspire. She sets the girls up with big sheets of paper on the dining table or at the artists' easel, and they have a stack of old cardboard egg cartons to use as paint palettes.

In the kitchen, a wall-mounted "check minder", such as you might find in a restaurant, is a child-friendly solution for displaying children's art. It gives the girls a quick and simple way of hanging their own pictures without using tape or tacks. Their prolific output of bold and bright paintings introduces a naive exuberance to their home.

ABOVE **Side-tables are the perfect scale for children. Fran and Barry picked up the original Ercol table nest at Ardingly antiques fair in Sussex and painted them in different colours.**

LEFT **When Fran's clothing samples arrive, there is a double dose of excitement. Anouk loves to see her mum's designs, while Ray plans a new cardboard playhouse.**

Fran developed her flair for colour through her career as a fashion designer for her clothing label Labour of Love. At home, she displays this instinctive eye for colour by combining a collection of hand-made beaded African fertility dolls from the 1950s with woven baskets and printed fabrics. The combination of ethnic artefacts and iconic pieces of mid-century furniture gives this home a unique spirit, and the girls can feed their imaginations surrounded by both primitive and modernist pieces.

ABOVE LEFT **A height chart is de rigueur in a children's room. It is always fascinating for them to look back at the rate at which they have grown. In time, this one can be detached from the wall, rolled up and stored in a memory box.**

LEFT **Brilliantly inventive storage is a key component of this home. In the bedroom the girls each have a spacious wardrobe with an enviable collection of clothes. The display of their clothes inspires endless dressing-up games.**

Anouk and Ray share a large bedroom that is divided by a shelving unit into sleeping quarters and a dress-up and play zone. Barry made much of the furniture himself and incorporated casters on most items. As the girls grow, the space can be transformed around them. What might have been a dark corner has been turned into a cosy den-like space for their bunk bed. On the far side of the room closer to the window, where there is plenty of light and space, they play. An unusual double desk, of French origin, takes centre stage when they play schools. Above it, layer upon layer of drawings and collages are pinned to a cork notice board. Every few months they pick out their favourite pieces and store them away in a portfolio, then start a new display.

The girls' bedroom is reminiscent of Fran's boutique, with neat rows of carefully curated clothes. Barry built large open units where things of beauty are put on display rather than hidden away. This is an easy space to keep organized and the numerous fabric prints and colours – works of art in themselves – create a colourful, fun environment. A door leads directly out to the garden, giving the children access to fresh air and outside play.

Fran puts the success of this home down to clever and hard-working design. Carefully thought out, the interior allows them time to focus on fun, creative and family activities.

THIS PAGE **Ray always takes great pride in adding her latest painting to the family art wall. The girls both have special painting T-shirts in their favourite colours instead of smocks or aprons.**

DENS, HIDEAWAYS AND PLAY ZONES

CHILDREN LEARN THROUGH CREATIVE PLAY. A DEN OR HIDEAWAY MAKES A GREAT BASE CAMP

WHERE THEY CAN HAVE ALL KINDS OF IMAGINARY ADVENTURES. FROM A SIMPLE CARDBOARD

BOX TO A RUSTIC-STYLE WOODEN SHACK, A DEN PROVIDES A PORTAL INTO ANOTHER WORLD.

BELOW **A den can be a solitary place where children get used to the idea of having their own space and spending time on their own. A hanging rattan chair, bang in the middle of the living room in Sonja's home, offers her children a quiet space. Make it cosy with a shearling throw and it will become a favourite spot for reading.**

RIGHT **Rasmus Frimer Andersen and Rasmus Skaarup, the architects who designed this family home for Thomas and Maiken, wanted to incorporate multi-functional design elements in the children's bedrooms. The deep box windowsills are the right height to double up as study desks. Dressed up with a pile of cushions, they turn into cool little hangouts.**

OPPOSITE **A temporary den is a good option for a family home where space can be tight. Adopt a nomadic spirit and invest in a teepee. This can be set up almost anywhere: at home, in the garden or the park or taken away on holiday. Here, the canvas has been customized with an outer fabric and crocheted patchwork cover.**

I have fond memories of the dens my sister and I made as children. Each one began as an imaginary world that became more and more elaborate. We made our simplest den out of sheets hanging from a tree in our garden, but our most exciting den was a cupboard on the landing. Our mum transformed it into a two-storey "house" by wedging an old teacher's desk inside it. My sister had the top half and I had the cave-like space at the bottom. Each den was given a name and became the base for a secret club. We invented secret codes, and made badges, members' cards and "Keep Out" signs.

Dens and hideaways provide children with perfect spaces for imaginary play. They are also ideal for games of hide and seek and as boltholes for having a nap or cosying up with a book. Whether it is simple or elaborate, create a den that will work within your space, and watch your children embrace it.

THIS PAGE AND OPPOSITE LEFT **Cardboard boxes** provide a great base for den-making. They won't be very long-lasting, but this doesn't matter, as they are built from readily available materials. Develop your ideas with each den that you create. Your children will love to get involved in the construction and, when they are old enough, they will be happy making a den by themselves.

RIGHT **If you don't want to construct a cardboard den, there are plenty of ready-made options, from rockets to houses. Buy a basic model and then customize it to suit your children. Better still, decorate it with them. Chloe upgraded a simple white structure with black sticky tape to make an exciting grocery store.**

BELOW RIGHT **A flattened box with a castellated silhouette and a drawbridge tied up with string is a simple DIY project. Prop it up inside a doorway and it will become the starting point for an afternoon of adventure. Put it out with your recycling and make something different next week.**

Den-building should be an everyday activity, like painting or playing, and every home is a potential base for the humblest of dens made from cardboard boxes. If you want to embrace the art of the DIY den, get into the habit of looking for suitable materials. The more you look, the more you will start to see the potential in everyday things such as discarded packing materials. I guarantee that you will soon find yourself arriving home with found materials for den-making on a regular basis. The joy of cardboard dens is that they don't last forever – the fact that they have a limited life span somehow adds to their magic. The fun is as much in the making as in the using, and each and every den you make will be better than the last one.

I love walking into a house and discovering something unexpected. Interior designer Sonja de Groot took inspiration from her son's love of climbing and hiding to create the ultimate bedroom den: "As soon as we saw the wooden beams in the attic bedroom, we thought it would be great to use them and to build a crow's nest for Sam (10)."

Alternatively, if you can find a solid beam in the ceiling or a suitable space in a doorway, consider adding a swing to a child's room. It will become the focal point of childhood games and provide endless hours of amusement. Blogger Monika Lenarczyk-Wiśniewska introduced a swing to her daughter's bedroom. "When the girls use the swing, sometimes they pretend they are performing in a circus. Other times they pretend that the swing is a stage. It feeds their imagination and keeps them happy for hours."

BELOW **Sonja and Eric** have created a crow's nest hideaway for their son Sam. It occupies the smallest space right at the top of his bedroom, between the roof beams. Sitting above a trap door, a climbing net doubles up as a way up and a safety net. It is the most exciting space in the house.

RIGHT **A permanent** structure can be a big investment in terms of both space and money. If you don't want to end up with a white elephant, you need to make it work for your family. Think about the different functions a den can perform. One that is large enough to accommodate a bedroll can be used as an invaluable sleepover space. My teenage nephew was the first person to spend a night in our shack (the outside can be seen opposite), and he gave it the thumbs up.

Dedicating some inside space to a den can sometimes provide you with unexpected options. We live in a converted factory building in East London and devoted some of our large open-plan space to a tiny house within a house. Our wooden shack sitting on casters can be pushed around the space as and when we wish. Truly multi-functional, it serves as my office, Olive's den for drawing and listening to music, a bunkhouse for kids' sleepovers and, when we have parties, it is transformed into a bar.

If you have limited space, you could invest in a fold-away den, easy and quick to put up and pull down. Lightweight, portable designs such as teepees or fabric wendy houses make it easy for kids to set up camp wherever they want. An inside bivouac will probably end up as a warm, comfy space filled with cushions and soft

THIS PAGE **If you plan to incorporate a permanent den into your living space, make sure it suits your interior style. Our bespoke shack is made out of reclaimed materials. The front panel, clad in upcycled floorboards, creates a giant chevron – our signature motif – that echoes the parquet flooring.**

toys – good for quiet reading or even an afternoon nap. An outdoor camp may become the focal point for more wild and raucous games.

We live near Hackney Marshes in London, a perfect den-making destination. Olive and her friends can spend whole afternoons absorbed in foraging for sticks and lengths of trailing ivy to make the perfect den. A combination of fresh air, problem-solving and creative thinking gives children a great sense of satisfaction. If you have a park or woodland close by, it won't be too difficult to find the raw materials you need without laying waste to trees and foliage. Den-making outside should be all about camouflage and blending into the landscape.

If you have outdoor space and a bigger budget, consider building a sturdy, watertight den or treehouse that can also be pressed into service for summer sleepovers. The flat roof of a wooden

LEFT **Silvia and Bartlomiej wanted to create a playful environment for Leo. By introducing elements from the outside, they have turned his bedroom into an exciting indoor playground. A solid door frame or beam can provide the perfect spot for attaching a swing. A series of mirror balls suspended like a constellation in front of the window reflects dancing light across the room as he swings.**

ABOVE **A swing gives children time for unstructured play when their imagination can wander into a world of make-believe. Swings also promote exercise, especially if it's a miserable day and your children are cooped up inside.**

OPPOSITE **A comfortable and cosy reading zone will encourage children to settle down with a good book.**

ABOVE **Making dens out of sticks is a fundamental part of childhood play. Stick-lets are a great invention. These reusable silicone joints make it really easy to assemble the framework for a den or teepee without having to tie or lash anything together. Keep a bag of Stick-lets close to hand for trips out to the forest or the park. They will give children a helping hand when it comes to constructing the perfect hideaway.**

playhouse can double up as a raised garden and provide a sunny spot for growing pots of herbs. Photographer Emma Donnelly sees lots of benefits in ten-year-old Monty and Agnes, aged seven, playing outside. "They love having a den in the back garden. It has encouraged them to play outside and to be inventive and imaginative with their own space. With so much technology about, there is something magical about old-fashioned play – it allows them to explore the world around them."

It's no surprise that all the best fairy tales feature hidden attics, cabins sited deep in the woods and mysterious caves. Small spaces can easily take on a magical quality and encourage your children's imaginations to run wild.

ABOVE **Dens made from old sheets were a daily feature during summers spent at our grandparents' house. We threw the sheets over the washing line and pinned them down with tent pegs. However, a garden isn't essential – a long length of fabric can be suspended indoors, with the ends anchored in place with piles of pillows.**

OPPOSITE **Emma and James live on the English coast where their children have lots of freedom to roam around in the fresh air. When they aren't playing in the beach hut in their back garden, they are out adventuring in their Canadian canoe.**

OPPOSITE **Agata and Ian had the notion of creating a little castle in the countryside for their family. Although their house isn't quite that grand, it is furnished with an appealing mix of reclaimed materials and antiques that gives their home an intriguing sense of history.**

RIGHT **In every corner of their home there are spaces that Bonnie can turn into dens. In the vestibule she can hide behind the curtains and turn it into a little room of her own, while the steps that lead down to the garden become a stage for jumping games.**

BELOW RIGHT **With a series of interlinked rooms, this is the perfect house for games of hide and seek. As the children grow, they will discover that there are even more hiding places, and Ian and Agata have already earmarked the cavernous basement as the ultimate pre-teen den.**

HOUSE OF SECRETS

FEATURE HOME

AGATA AND IAN HAMILTON HAVE TRANSFORMED A HISTORIC HOUSE ON THE OUTSKIRTS OF WARSAW INTO A RAMBLING FAMILY HOME. BUILT IN 1900 AS A SECRET LOVERS' HIDEAWAY, IT IS NOW A PLAYFUL ENVIRONMENT FOR THE COUPLE AND THEIR CHILDREN, BONNIE, AGED FOUR, AND HUGO, THREE MONTHS. BY COMBINING THEIR POLISH AND ENGLISH BACKGROUNDS WITH A LOVE OF ARCHITECTURE AND AN INHERITED COLLECTION OF ANTIQUES, AGATA AND IAN HAVE CREATED THEIR OWN UNIQUE MODERN FAMILY STYLE.

BELOW The big Balinese table in Bonnie's art studio was inherited from the former owner. And while Agata says it wouldn't have been their choice, it is the perfect height and size for a big group of children. When Bonnie isn't sitting at it painting or drawing, she can jump and dance on top of it. According to Bonnie, the best thing about it is being able to hide underneath it.

RIGHT A teepee could be the emblem for this house of hideaways and dens. The miniature version is a nod to nomadic rustic life and to the vision of freedom that Ian and Agata are creating for their children. A row of painted cupboards has been turned into a giant chalkboard.

FAR RIGHT When children are worn out, they need comforting places where they can curl up for a daytime nap. Agata turned squares of foam into giant patchwork cushions. Light and comfortable, they can be carried from room to room and turn any corner into a cosy space.

Creating a dynamic space for their children to grow up in was high on Agata and Ian's list of priorities. Their original vision to convert an old barn into a family home initially drew a blank because old buildings are in short supply in and around Warsaw. By broadening their search to include derelict houses, they discovered a place close to Agata's childhood home. The old house offered an ideal project and allowed the couple to focus their attention and passion on an extensive renovation job. Restoring the run-down structure not only enabled them to embrace the character and soul of the building, but also provided scope for incorporating their own ideas for modern family living.

The interior of their home pays homage to the couple's shared passions and it comes as no surprise to learn that Agata and Ian are both designers. The industrial edge to the interior contrasts with the surrounding countryside and the rustic features of the house. There is a very real sense that this is a working home, where the kitchen table provides space for creative projects as well as a place for the family to congregate at meal times.

Agata and Ian both thrive in the atmosphere of creative studio life and have incorporated a studio for the children too. This seemed as natural to them as providing a playroom. It is the children's domain

THIS PAGE **Give children the basics and they will create their own games. You don't need to be overly prescriptive with your playhouse design. Ian built this simple wooden frame for Bonnie. It can be anything she imagines — a house, a shop, a hospital or a café.**

LEFT AND RIGHT **The black walls and grey concrete floor in the big kitchen create a dramatic space where Bonnie loves to play. Chalking games of hopscotch is a regular event in this house. In the winter months, when snow is thick on the ground outside, under-floor heating turns the kitchen into a snug retreat. Under a column of Bonnie's drawings, there is an empty space for her to chalk something new everyday.**

and is at the heart of the house. The concrete floor, rusted-steel beam and exposed brickwork give the space an industrial feel, and one of the walls has become a home for Bonnie's painted canvases. Agata and Ian constructed a wooden "house" to serve as a multi-purpose play space for Bonnie. The simple frame, easily adapted with different fabrics, can become a playhouse, a den or a shop, depending on the game of the day. The plan is to add casters to make it mobile and thus even more adaptable.

The renovation is an ongoing vehicle for Agata and Ian and is far from finished. In places, instead of doors, they have heavy drapes hanging in the doorways, and these add to the transient spirit of a house that is full of constantly evolving ideas. The addition of two new rooms on the ground floor has created a free-flowing circular route through the house. Bonnie and her friends, on foot or on scooter, can speed from room to room without ever reaching a dead end. It is a road that leads to endless adventures.

The layers of history have been preserved in a sensitive way here, with original materials, such as exposed brick and wood, creating an atmosphere of rustic warmth. The polished concrete kitchen floor, coloured with dark grey pigment, provides textural contrast. Bonnie uses this space as a play area and likes to chalk pictures and graffiti on the dark floor. The chalkboard walls are used too, and both can easily be wiped clean.

BELOW Bonnie has an antique double bed that is a platform for all sorts of games. The bed had been stored away in pieces by the previous owner of the house, but its original dark-stained wood meant this rather sombre piece of furniture was ripe for restoration. Painting it duck egg blue revived it and gave it a new character.

LEFT AND ABOVE It's the hideaway spaces under the eaves that make Bonnie's room an exciting place to be. In a home where den-making is the order of the day, she pilfers cushions from every room in the house to furnish her spaces. It's a sure thing that her creative skills will become more and more sophisticated as she gets older.

FAMILY Q&A

What is your family motto?
Live and let live.

Describe your family in three words:
Dreamers, makers, eaters.

Ian, have you kept anything from your childhood?
My trunk from boarding school, with all of my school reports and letters to family.

What did you enjoy doing as a child?
I always lived in the countryside, so we made dens in barns, hollow trees and outhouses. It was a big part of my childhood.

Agata, what is the key for a happy childhood?
Giving children love and security, and a base that they can always call home.

You are passionate about giving Bonnie a creative environment. What are the most important provisions you make?
We try not to restrict her by setting up a relaxed environment and we let Bon explore with her art activities. We feel very lucky
because we have enough space to give her freedom.

Why do you think Bonnie is such a prolific little creator?
I think the process of seeing us build the house and then decorate each space has given her a sense of making/doing/ creating/discussing.

Has Bonnie helped with any of the renovation projects?
The big wooden table in her room had some broken legs. She helped the builder repair them so she has an attachment to the piece and still remembers that work. She also helped me to paint her bed.

Bonnie, what is your favourite game?
Building dens!

What do you like chalking on the kitchen floor?
Very, very long hopscotch boards.

Do you have a favourite hiding place?
In the studio, under the old wooden table.

Upstairs, the children's bedrooms feel like snug hiding places. Hugo's cot fits neatly into a cosy, specially built alcove trimmed with cabin-like timber cladding. Bonnie's bedroom, tucked away neatly under the eaves, is a series of cleverly conceived, cosy, den-like spaces. Instead of enclosing the old building's nooks and crannies, they have been left open, giving the children the opportunity and flexibility to transform the spaces themselves as they grow. A pretty canopy of fabrics has transformed Bonnie's antique bed into a dreamy, fairy-tale retreat.

The house has a rather grand presence, but there is nothing stuffy or formal in the way this family lives. Instead, this is a home where spontaneity and a spirit of play is encouraged.

CREATIVE SPACES AND HOMEWORK ZONES

IT ISN'T A NECESSITY FOR CHILDREN TO HAVE A DEDICATED CREATIVE OR
HOMEWORK ZONE, BUT IT IS WORTH CONSIDERING WHAT YOU CAN PROVIDE
WITHIN THE SPACE THAT YOU HAVE. AS CHILDREN GROW, THEIR NEEDS WILL
INCREASE, SO KEEP AN EYE OPEN FOR CLEVER IDEAS TO ADAPT YOUR HOME.

THIS PAGE AND OPPOSITE
BELOW LEFT An old school desk
can turn the corner of a bedroom
into a buzzy little area. Anouk and
Ray love to sit at their double desk
and play schools. It is a space
where they can express themselves
through creative role play.

RIGHT **Monika and Emil encourage their children to play games at the dining table. They have places to play in their shared bedroom, but being in the open-plan living space means the family can be together even if Monika and Emil are cooking.**

For little children, sticking, painting and colouring are all about getting messy, rolling up their sleeves and playing with colour and texture. All they need are the basic materials, as much space as possible and lots of encouragement. When Olive was small, we didn't set aside a specific space for painting. We would simply roll out a wipeable oilcloth on the kitchen floor and cover it with lining paper. It gave us scope to paint on a large scale without worrying about things falling off the edge of a table.

Mother of four Linda Hamrin Tait enjoys seeing her children absorbed in creative activities. "Oliver (5) and Astrid (7) love creating. After school, they spread their paper and paints out on our dining-room table.

Elin (3) loves to join in and I can imagine the fun when Ida (6 months) is a bit older. At the moment they all gravitate to being together. I don't think they need their own space at the moment – there is plenty of time for that."

When Olive was younger, we enjoyed painting or drawing side by side. I always resisted the temptation to take over and instead tried to encourage her to develop her own ideas. As soon as her paintings had dried, we stuck them straight up on

LEFT The shack is my workspace during the day. When Olive comes home from school, I am happy to move out to give her some space to do her homework. She loves to close up the front and hide away, listening to music while she is drawing.

the wall next to the table. I have often wondered what the effect would be of sitting back and watching rather than directing and guiding. Hearing Olive's art teacher say that at 12 she is already developing her own style has answered my question. Encourage, facilitate and engage, then let your children do the rest.

We all know that as children grow, they learn about the world through play. They replay events of the day and act out scenarios. Playing schools is a popular game and a desk is the number one prop. Used in different ways, it can transform into a shop counter, the bridge of a ship or a table in a café. There are beautifully designed desks, made from sustainable products, that adapt as your children grow. They come with a price tag, but they will last more than

OPPOSITE An old-fashioned knee-hole office desk makes a neat and affordable homework base for a pre-teen. They are easy enough to pick up on eBay or at yard sales. If you are lucky enough, you might find one with a key for a drawer, which will add an element of excitement and secrecy.

THIS PAGE **Sonja and Eric** have come up with a simple solution for turning their coveted Herman Ypma desks in the living room into an intimate space: a white curtain draws across the room, dividing it in two. This also provides a spare room whenever they need it.

a lifetime and turn into a suitable space for homework later on. If you are on a tighter budget, there are plenty of basic options that will last until they have been outgrown. Try searching on eBay or in second-hand stores for vintage office desks. They are usually made of stronger stuff than many modern pieces of furniture and often have exciting hidden pen compartments and inkwells that children love.

If you have your own desk or workspace at home, you can be sure that it will become a favourite place for your children to play. Interior designer Sonja de Groot embraces the children's love of working at her desk. "Sam (10) and Lieve (7) both have workspaces in their bedrooms, but because they like to be with us, they often work at the desks in the living room. I enjoy having the kids working in here with us and being able to stimulate their creativity."

When the homework schedule starts to kick in, it is probably time to revamp your child's work zone, but you don't need to overthink it. Journalist Ewa Solarz had a really simple solution: "When Jasiek (12) started school, we divided the desk in his room with red tape – a playing zone and tidy scholar zone."

ABOVE **A child-sized desk creates a little place of focus even for young children. Monika chose a retro-inspired Formica desk and chair for her daughters to share. The little drawer is the perfect place for keeping drawing paper and pens.**

RIGHT **If you have the space in your living room, the addition of a children's table will serve many different purposes. This simple wooden table is big enough for two friends to sit opposite each other and play. It can double up as a children's dinner table and can easily be carried out into the garden in the summer.**

RIGHT AND BELOW **Whenever Anete has a vision for their home, she searches high and low until she finds something that fits the bill. Old-fashioned school desks were high on the list of priorities for Kaya and Zuza. It seems appropriate that she found the twins a double vintage desk where they can sit side by side. When the girls want to spread out, they sit up at the big dining-room table.**

THIS PAGE **Nina works from home and is happy to share her workspace with her children. A row of simple white tables gives them enough space to sit in the attic office together. The children each have a brightly coloured cork notice board where they can pin their drawings.**

THIS PAGE A built-in work bench is often the best way to maximize your space. Ewa and Milosz wanted Marianna and Jasiek to have a decent desk space in their own rooms. The big picture windows give them the backdrop of the trees in their garden and flood their desks with natural light.

ABOVE **The windowsill behind Jasiek's desk is lined with an impressive collection of cacti. As long as children are aware of their sharp needles, they are easy to look after.**

Don't overlook the space you have outside. Painting a section of outside wall with chalkboard paint turns a redundant space into a creative one. If you have a paved area outside, keep a box of chalks at the ready. I used to love sitting on our front steps while Olive and her friends chalked up and down the length of our block. Photographer Emma Donnelly sees the potential for creativity in their back garden: "In the summer, Monty (10) and Agnes (7) use the back garden as an extension for their play and crafting. They always prefer to be outside and their wooden playhouse has been a café and art studio!"

Seize any opportunity to facilitate creative activities. Even bath time can take a creative route with special bath crayons. And any plan that combines daily routines with creativity is a winner.

BELOW An abundance of suitable storage is a prerequisite for a large family. The entire length of a wall lined with Ikea Expedit cupboards provides an endless number of compartments. The individual boxy spaces make it easy to stack possessions in piles of a manageable size.

RIGHT Chloe and Tom's fun-loving spirit serves them well as parents to four children. When a dolls' house arrived last Christmas, Chloe spent hours decorating it and making miniature versions of their own furniture and posters. The children asked if Father Christmas had really brought it for her.

HOUSE OF PLENTY

CHILDHOOD SWEETHEARTS CHLOE AND TOM THURSTON HAVE A LAID-BACK APPROACH TO FAMILY LIFE. RATHER THAN SPENDING TIME AGONIZING ABOUT THE PERFECT FAMILY HOME, THEY BOUGHT A NEW BUILD THAT THEY COULD EASILY MAKE THEIR OWN. THEY LOVE TO TRAVEL WITH BELLA, AGED ELEVEN, NINE-YEAR-OLD SATCHEL, FOUR-YEAR-OLD KITTY AND RAFFERTY, ONE, AND ARE SECURE IN THE KNOWLEDGE THAT THEY HAVE A BASE TO COME HOME TO. CHLOE AND TOM PREVIOUSLY LIVED IN IBIZA WITH BELLA AND SATCHEL, AND NOW THEY ARE HATCHING PLANS TO MOVE THE WHOLE FAMILY TO MALLORCA.

The Thurstons' super-cool, fun-loving modern home is just five minutes from the beach in Dorset, where the couple both grew up. Chloe is a blogger and Tom is an app developer, and they are both great believers in empowering their children with a mastery of technology. The oldest three children have desks in their rooms, but two work stations equipped with giant Macs are designated for family use and are the most popular seats in the house. However,

THIS PAGE **Two Beståburs Ikea desks placed side by side have turned this work station into mission control. It's a hotbed of techno-creativity for a new generation. The white high-gloss desks and the Uten.Silo wall storage unit give it a fun space-age vibe.**

Chloe and Tom have an unwritten rule that screen time shouldn't interrupt real life and pride themselves in teaching their children to use technology in a creative rather than compulsive way. You won't catch any of the children on their devices on family trips or at meal times.

Chloe has a love of minimalist style, but with four children she admits defeat. Instead, she has adopted a philosophy of a simple white background that can take pops of colour and graphic posters. The house is overflowing with beautifully designed kids' products, but the family really enjoys Chloe's much-loved childhood collection of vintage books and toys. These take pride of place and Chloe avidly scours eBay to add to her 1980s collections of My Little Pony and Care Bears. Storage is an absolute essential in this family home. Luckily they have plenty of custom-built storage where they can stash things away if they want a speedy clear-up.

LEFT **A graphic mix of monochrome prints and bed linen turns Satchel's bed into a modern-day superhero's hangout. An assortment of Lego storage boxes fits neatly under his bed.**

BELOW **If you have a big family, make life easy with mix-and-match bed linen. A collection of black-and-white prints means any combination works and, more importantly, bedtime is always a surprise.**

LEFT **A hall is the perfect space for a gallery wall. Another of Chloe's projects is to customize Frames wallpaper from Graham & Brown. She fills the frames with printouts of black-and-white illustrations. Whether you choose to introduce colour or go the monochrome route, you could turn this into a family art project. Let your children draw directly into the frames, or cut templates for them to draw on and create a totally unique wallpaper.**

The house is spacious enough to allow an open-plan layout on the ground floor. Their theory is that by living in a physically open space, the family will develop a culture of openness. By being in the same space most of the time, Chloe and Tom are really in touch with the kids. They can spread out and enjoy the space, even if they aren't doing things together.

Tom is teaching Bella and Satchel computer-coding and how to make computer-generated music. Chloe set them up with a private blog on WordPress so that they could experiment with publishing. Bella and her friends have started a website selling T-shirts they have designed with computer-generated transfers of their drawings, while Satchel picks up tips from art and magic trick tutorials on YouTube. When they have homework, they can commandeer a Mac each. There isn't an official screen-time limit when they are working on homework or creative activities, but they are only allowed to play computer games one evening each weekend.

For simplicity's sake, there is now a "majority rule" approach in this home, as accommodating the individual interests of four children became a logistical nightmare. Three children would end up sitting outside a judo hall or a dance studio waiting for one child to finish their activity. Now they all spend time together as a family unless at least three of them want to do the same thing. Downtime in their busy schedule is something the whole family enjoys, and it also gives them a sense of balance. The children are a great team and there is plenty of time for them to set technology aside and be kids. They spend

THIS PAGE **If you are the eldest child in a busy family home, it can be important to have a bolthole. Bella has a neat area in her bedroom where she can work or play. A cleverly designed trestle table from Ikea can be tilted to turn into a drawing board.**

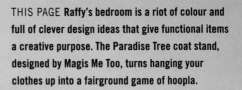

THIS PAGE **Raffy's bedroom is a riot of colour and full of clever design ideas that give functional items a creative purpose. The Paradise Tree coat stand, designed by Magis Me Too, turns hanging your clothes up into a fairground game of hoopla.**

hours in the garden playing energetic games, larking around and putting on entertaining shows. When Tom and Chloe have work trips, they all travel as a family.

Upstairs, the kids have light, airy rooms that work on the same principle as downstairs – white walls with a graphic injection of posters and wall hangings. Bella has a room to herself where she likes to spend time alone. It has a grown-up air about it, with a large trestle table, her Polaroid camera and a favourite stationery stash. Only the neat row of Sonny Angel dolls reminds you that this isn't a teenager's room. Satchel and Kitty share a bedroom below the eaves. It's big enough to allow them a generous corner and a window each. Satchel has a simple desk that he uses as a work station for making Lego models. Having his own space gives him the option to suit himself. Kitty likes to use her vintage wooden desk and pretty pink chair for all her imaginary games.

Chloe and Tom embrace exciting technological advances without sacrificing the simplicity of their favourite childhood things. Family closeness and plenty of fresh air are the magic ingredients that counteract the computer wizardry to provide a healthy life balance.

ABOVE LEFT **Happy is the order of the day in Raffy's rainbow-themed bedroom. Inflatables, such as hot-air balloons, crocodiles and palm trees, introduce an element of fun to a child's room and make great props for games. Add a series of hooks to the ceiling so that you can introduce new elements. Inflatables are so lightweight** that you can simply unhook them for playtime.

ABOVE RIGHT **A masked wooden coat hanger from Red Hand Gang turns Raffy's gilet into a kooky character on his bedroom wall. His Brio stove is a hit when it comes to making pizzas to be sold in the cardboard grocery store downstairs.**

FAMILY Q&A

What is your family motto?
Choose a job you love and never work again. This is something we really try to instil and encourage in the kids.

Describe your family in three words:
Fun, energetic and hectic!

Chloe, when did you meet Tom?
We lived next door to each other when we were growing up. We were best friends and Tom cut a hole in the fence so that we could see each other in the garden.

Tom, do you have any rules around screen time?
Our kids know when it is appropriate and when it isn't. With a busy house they don't get the chance to do any one thing for too long. We would never let them have devices during meals or at a restaurant. They know that it shouldn't interrupt any real-life experiences.

Chloe, do you have any favourite children's books?
I have always wanted to complete my sets of 1980s Care Bears and

My Little Pony books. I find missing books on eBay but my old ones are the best... they still have my initials written in them.

Chloe, do you spend much time with your parents?
They live nearby and we are always at my parents' pool in the summer.

Bella, what do you like using the computer for?
Working on my shop, Panda Aliens.

Satchel, what is your favourite thing to do on the computer?
Making music (Satch wants to be a superstar DJ!).

Kitty, where do you like to play when you are at home?
My room, because I love it.

Kitty, what is the best thing in your dolls' house?
The mini blankets, because I love putting the Sonny Angels to bed.

Raffy, what is your favourite word?
Roar!

SNUG BEDROOMS

TAKE AN IMAGINATIVE APPROACH TO
DESIGNING A CHILD'S BEDROOM AND
CREATE A SPECIAL SPACE THAT HAS
HEART AND SOUL. EVEN THE SIMPLEST
OF SPACES CAN BE TRANSFORMED
TO PROVIDE YOUR CHILDREN WITH
A SENSE OF WARMTH AND SECURITY.

BELOW Silvia has an open mind about how Leo's bedroom is going to develop, but she is clear that she wants to create a playful space that reflects his personality. She has lots of ideas to share with him as he gets older, but she acknowledges that his opinion is key.

RIGHT Monika has created a fun bedroom for Zoja, Bianka and Gaia to share. Gaia's bed and cloud-shaped rug were both made by Polish design duo Kutikai. A large, traditional armoire, updated by Woodszczescia with a coat of mint green paint, houses all the girls' clothes plus their dancewear from Monika's own label Girls On Tiptoes.

OPPOSITE Hugo's nursery has an unexpected combination of rustic elements and colour. Almost everything Agata and Ian own comes with a story; for example, this is their favourite rug, bought from an Arab market. Instead of a designer cot/crib, they bought an Ikea model. Customized with VOC-free paint, you too can turn a standard design into a statement piece.

Children's bedrooms should be snug and cosy with the primary focus on story time and bedtime. With some careful planning, you can create a room that becomes a playroom by day and a bedroom by night.

If you don't have a room for a separate nursery, you can adapt your bedroom to have a little zone for your baby. A corner or an alcove can be turned into a beautiful, simple space with a cot/crib and a mobile. Add some pretty lightweight hanging fabric and you will create a softly lit recess. If you do have a spare room, putting together a nursery is without doubt the most exciting interior project for most parents. Choose adaptable pieces of furniture that can grow with your children. There are products for every budget – the key is to avoid buying nursery paraphernalia that you can live without. Illustrator Silvia Pogoda likes the simplicity in her 18-month-old son Leo's room. "He is still too small to tell me what he likes, so for now I use my imagination and try to look at things with the eyes of a small child."

When my daughter Olive was a baby, I kept things simple. A chest of drawers stationed beneath the stairs made a cosy nook for her change table.

If you can resist the temptation to buy too many pieces of clothing, it will be much less demanding on your space. When we were children, we had what we needed – one to wash, one to wear and one to air. I believe one large drawer should be adequate for a layette. Add a row of hooks to display your favourite pieces.

Atmospheric lighting is the simplest way to change the environment from a bright and cheery play zone to a serene place of slumber. Dimmer switches are the most obvious solution, but there is something magical about a nightlight that only comes on at bedtime.

THIS PAGE **Raffy's toddler bed is the base camp for all kinds of games, as well as being a dreamy place to sleep. When he sits on the front of the wheeled bed, he uses his lively imagination to turn it into a car or a bus.**

BRIO.

10®

The paper bag®

This bag is made from recycled paper. It is 100% natural. 180 g/m² double-layer white kraft layered with brown kraft. Capacity: 33 litres. 100% Ecographik.® Do not throw it away. It is reusable.

PIZZA-PARTY

BELOW Decorating a room in bright or bold colours isn't the only way to give it character. A collage of black-and-white posters stuck to the wall with monochrome washi tape turns a white space into a giant comic-book statement.

RIGHT Beds should be comfy places that can be used at playtime as well as bedtime – a heap of colourful pillows can transform a bed into a sultan's palace or a sky full of fluffy clouds. When children put their own toys to bed each evening, it can be a useful way to begin the winding-down process of getting them ready for their own bedtime.

BOTTOM RIGHT The folksy styling of Bianka's Mofflo bed is reminiscent of designs from traditional children's storybooks. Painted in a soft pink hue, it has a dreamy quality. The solid wooden frame makes it a comfortable place to sit and read, and also means that things don't disappear down the back of the bed.

Many of the children in this book share bedrooms with their siblings. Blogger Monika Lenarczyk-Wiśniewska has created a bedroom that Zoja (6), Bianka (4) and Gaia (2) share. "I chose a different style of bed for each of my children. It has helped to create the feeling of different areas that suit their individual personalities." Bunk beds are a classic space-saving option, and I have met families whose children co-sleep very happily in their infant years. Beds that incorporate storage make good use of

THIS PAGE **Chloe and Tom commissioned a carpenter to custom-build a wooden bed frame for Kitty. The silhouette of the house fits neatly over a junior mattress. At bedtime the string of lights attached to the roof creates a lovely glow. At playtime the frame can be draped with fabrics, transforming it into an exciting playhouse.**

THIS PAGE **Agnes's bedroom is a rich and cheerful patchwork of colour and print. With a mix of geometrics and illustrations, it doesn't have a rigid theme, but it does make sure that her space is a spontaneous reflection of the things she likes.**

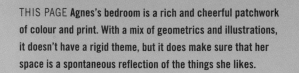

ABOVE I found it impossible to find anything labelled with my name when I was growing up, but with the trend for all kinds of vintage-inspired letters, it's now easy to pick out an initial. Illuminated letters might not suit every budget, but this giant "A" adds a touch of circus excitement to Agnes's bedroom.

RIGHT Agata made a simple fabric canopy to transform Bonnie's bed into a fairy-tale space, suspending the material by way of a curtain pole attached to the ceiling. The addition of a string of lights turns it into a wonderland at night time.

small spaces. Bedrooms that look more like toy shops don't promote bedtime, so being able to clear the decks at the end of the day is a big plus. If there isn't time for Olive and me to tidy her room before bedtime, I sneak back in and do a quick whip round when she is asleep. It means a new day can start without feeling chaotic from the get-go.

We are temporarily living in a one-bedroom cottage while we renovate our East London factory. It's a very different style of living,

so we have had to be inventive with the limited space available and make the most of it, especially when it comes to sleeping arrangements. We have turned a built-in closet into a kind of wooden cabin to accommodate the head of Olive's bed. Draped with makeshift curtains, it has become an exciting space where Olive feels as though she is bunking down in a tent. We are here for a six-month stint and I am sure it will lose its attraction, but for now it feels like an adventure.

ABOVE **A multi-purpose duo of tables is a smart addition to a pre-teen's room. A nest of vintage coffee tables from eBay would make a great project to upcycle with an older child. Pick their three favourite colours and paint the top of each table in a different one.**

LEFT **When children develop a love of a particular colour, it's high time to let them style their own room. Selma's striking collection of yellow and purple furnishings has stamped her own signature onto her space.**

OPPOSITE **Let your children's passions lead the way when you design a space for them. Sonja and Eric embraced their son Sam's love of climbing and worked an activity space into his bedroom. A simple low-level bed creates an illusion of space in his attic room.**

LEFT AND RIGHT **Family heirlooms don't have to be things of monetary value. In fact, they can have far more meaning if they just carry sentimental value. The sailing ship displayed on a shelf in Monty's room was a labour of love made by his great-grandfather in the 1960s. The individual pieces arrived week by week with a modelling magazine he subscribed to, and before he added the sails, his wife stained them a more authentic colour using tea leaves. Monty is a nature lover and a member of the sea scouts, and he likes to use his microscope to look at bugs and shells collected on his excursions.**

OPPOSITE **The most striking bedrooms contain handmade elements. Emma made a wall hanging from some driftwood collected from their local beach, adding magpie and pheasant feathers from Monty's collection.**

Cabin-style and platform beds cross into den territory and can be exciting spaces for children. In a small room, they free up valuable child-height floor space that can be used for all kinds of adventure games. But I can't help thinking that a simple divan/box spring bed is much cosier when it comes to cuddling up at story time and (when needs must) drifting off to sleep next to your children.

If you have enough space, divide a child's bedroom into a den-like sleeping zone and a bigger, brighter play zone. Simple pigeonhole shelving units, such as ones sold by Ikea, work well as room dividers – they double up as storage and don't block too much light. If you want to find something a bit quirkier or more individual, try searching for vintage retro-style furniture on eBay.

RIGHT **Kaya and Zuza have two doors that lead into their bedroom. One is off the hall and the other is from their parents' bedroom. It gives them a fun circular route when they want to run around and play, and at the weekends it creates an intimate space where they can all lie in bed and talk to each other.**

THIS PAGE **Kaya and Zuza are lucky enough to be able to choose bedding from their mum's bedding label, Lola y Lolo. Their individual tastes give each of the twin Ikea beds its own distinctive style.**

ABOVE **Olive's room was inspired by her love of surf shacks and a holiday in a rustic retreat in the Sierra de Cazorla in southern Spain. Heavy handwoven Mexican throws used as curtains block out the light and add some soul to her room. The vibrant colours pop against the matt black wall and give her room a hint of pre-teen drama.**

RIGHT **Some of the most creative ideas happen by accident. Anete's father miscalculated how much wallpaper they needed for the twins' room. Instead of rushing out to buy more, Anete ran with a decoupage idea by cutting out some of the birds, butterflies and dragonflies and sticking them around the door frame.**

As children get older, it's important to involve them in the design of their own rooms. Photographer Emma Donnelly was inspired by her son's love of birds. "When Monty (10) asked for a stuffed bird for his eighth birthday, we contacted a local taxidermist. Monty wasn't expecting such a magnificent bird and it has made his room into a special place."

Even at the age of four, Olive used to rearrange her room and I found it fascinating to see where her imagination led her. Get down to look at things from your children's level – it's their space, so simple decisions, like hanging pictures on walls at the right height for them, can make a world of difference.

HOUSE OF DREAMS

WHEN NINA NÄGEL AND SIMON PACKER WANTED TO CREATE A SPACIOUS FAMILY HOME, THEY SOLD THEIR HIP URBAN LOFT IN EAST LONDON AND BOUGHT AN IMPRESSIVE FIVE-STOREY VICTORIAN HOME IN SOUTH-EAST LONDON FOR THEIR FAMILY TO GROW INTO. JAKOB (SIX), LEO (THREE) AND ALEXA (TEN MONTHS) HAVE A BEDROOM EACH, AND THERE IS STILL ENOUGH SPACE FOR NINA TO RUN HER BUSINESS FROM HOME.

LEFT **I love to see the resurgence of old-fashioned ideas. There are lots of contemporary versions of pegboards on the market with clips and hooks that make great family notice boards, but you can also buy traditional pegboard by the sheet to create your own custom-made organizer.**

Nina had a colourful and exciting childhood in Hamburg, where her mum, Graziela Preiser, worked as a magazine editor, art director and illustrator. In the 1970s and '80s, Graziela produced illustrations for her own range of fabrics, bedding and china, and became a household name in Germany. It comes as no surprise that, growing up surrounded by her mum's designs, Nina also has a passion for print and colour. She studied graphic design and then ran a studio with a partner for seven years. The resurgence of retro

THIS PAGE **A pile of luxurious blankets in the living room is always at the ready if the children want to take an afternoon nap. When the boys are running around playing lively games, they can be requisitioned as superhero capes.**

BELOW **Give your children time and a space to play together around a big table – this can be less restricting than sitting down to a child-sized desk. Nina often spreads out giant sheets of paper on the dining table for the boys to collaborate on colouring projects.**

RIGHT **A row of low-level Stuva storage units from Ikea sits neatly under the large bay window. Full of Lego building blocks, this light and sunny space has become a favourite spot where the boys enjoy making and displaying their models.**

FAR RIGHT **There is no need to buy expensive matching nursery furniture. This Ikea trolley currently houses baby essentials, but in later years Alexa could turn it into a triple bunk for her favourite toys or it could find a new life in the kitchen.**

style and the arrival of her own children inspired Nina to relaunch her mum's designs. Renamed byGraziela, the label has gained a cult following with parents who remember the patterns from their own childhoods.

The ground floor of Nina and Simon's family home is expansive enough for them to capture the spirit of open-plan living. Having a large communal living space was important to them, as they wanted to retain the feeling of togetherness and family time that they enjoyed so much in their first home.

For anything to find its way into this space, it has to pass the test of working for all the family. The children have an assortment of toy boxes to hold their things, but they do not look overly "kiddie" and sit well in an adult environment. Nina and Simon love modern furniture, but they don't take it too seriously and combine it with fun accessories that tell a story. When their taste differs, they are tolerant of each other and that makes the house feel like a genuine and soulful home. For example, Simon's racing trophy could easily have been a thorn in Nina's side; instead, it takes pride of place on their mantelpiece in an arrangement that says, simply, "family".

Upstairs, the abundance of bedrooms meant they were spoiled for choice when it came to deciding who should sleep where. All of the rooms have grand proportions and each of them has its own

THIS PAGE **As the third child in the family, Alexa has lots of hand-me-downs, but it hasn't stopped Nina from revamping the nursery for her. The cot/crib is in its third lifecycle, but has been given an update with a new mattress and bumper.**

ABOVE LEFT AND RIGHT **Nina** has lots of creative ideas that make her children's bedrooms unique. Rather than buying standard shelving for Jakob's knick-knacks, she collected a trio of wooden display houses on eBay. They were rather fiddly to paint, so she took the clever and easy option and decided to spray them, using three key shades that pick up on the signature colours in the bold retro fabrics that her mum has designed.

LEFT **When Simon met Nina, one** of his first gifts to her was a giant wall-sized appliquéd map of the world. It came with a collection of Velcro labels and symbolic items that represented different countries. This was an inspired and unusual way of saying "Let's travel the world together". Today it hangs on the wall in Jakob's room and is the perfect way of passing on the spirit of wanderlust. Twice the size of him, it has fed his geographical curiosity and now he knows the names of many more countries than most children his age and has a list of countries he wants to explore.

unique quality, but in some ways the boys have the best rooms in the house. Jakob's room is spacious enough for a complete train track and giant soft-play cubes to be left out ready for playtime. He also has stacks of storage to house his ever-growing collection of Lego. The Ikea bed has been transformed from a regulation, slightly clunky piece of furniture into a fun storage solution by spelling out "LEGO" in washi tape on the two deep drawers underneath. Leo's room gets the most sun, and Nina often plays there with Alexa while he is at nursery.

Prints from byGraziela have turned the children's bedrooms into cheerful spaces with an abundance of squashy cushions, colourful bed linen and framed posters. Seeing the boys playing imaginative games inspired by the illustrations brings back memories of her own creative childhood for Nina.

Nina and Simon have focused on creating a nurturing environment for the children, even if that means making some concessions. Despite their instinctive urge to rip up the beige fitted carpets, they decided to keep them until the children are older.

BELOW The creativity that Nina shares with her mum is easy to see in the handcrafted items around the home. In the 1980s Nina's mum made a series of painted wooden chairs in the shape of animals. They are the perfect childhood companions and their handmade quality gives them real originality. Jakob and Leo each have a chair that they treasure as being something made by their grandma.

THIS PAGE **Leo's bedroom is a riot of colour that pays homage to his grandma's playful spirit. The classic designs that Nina also had in her childhood bedroom look as fresh today as they did then. Leo has a mix of new and vintage toys that he loves in equal measure.**

FAMILY Q&A

What is your family motto?
Laugh and learn, dream and discover and, if all fails, bada bing, bada boom!

Describe your family in three words:
Organized, crazy, happy.

Nina, what is the key to a happy childhood?
Actively encouraging creativity as well as giving a lot of freedom. Also, it helps to buy new colouring pens now and again, as all the lids keep going missing!

Do you have any tips for designing a child's bedroom?
Find a balance between functionality and design. The oversized Lego bricks that Jakob uses for storage in his bedroom are a great example.

Who makes the decisions about the things in your home?
A lot of things in our home are from photoshoots from my work. I just bought a big yellow hare and he now sits happily on our mantelpiece. New drawings by the children appear, so it's always a process of change!

Do you like making things for your home?
Yes, at the moment I am crocheting lots of funny decorations.

Simon, what do you remember most about your own bedroom as a child?
The koala print wallpaper.

Are there any similarities between the boys' childhood and your own?
Yes, a love of Lego.

Jakob, what do you like to collect?
Match Attax cards, Kinder Egg toys and Star Wars figures.

What do you like best about your bedroom?
Being quiet and reading.

What is your favourite colour?
Red and blue and white because they are the Bayern Munich soccer kit colours.

Leo, what games do you like to play?
I love playing trains, going to the park and racing my scooter around the kitchen table with my brother.

OPPOSITE **Children are influenced by their surroundings and naturally learn new things every day. Very young children don't require structured learning, but simply need to be given the space to play and explore. Leo's bedroom is a colourful display of animals, vehicles, letters and words, which paints an inspiring picture of a home that celebrates learning through play. He is engaged in the things around him that give rise to all kinds of games and childhood curiosity.**

BELOW **Feed your children's imagination with motifs and quirky room decor. Black vinyl stars scattered on Leo's white bedroom wall evoke the sense of a snow-covered landscape. The vinyl triangles on the drawers below become snowy mountains – the perfect habitat for the funny moose that watches over him when he is sleeping.**

When the boys rough and tumble on the carpet, it is obvious that it is a much more comfortable surface for lively play than a wooden floor.

Alexa's nursery is an unexpected and playful combination of colours and prints. The cloud motif on the roller blind and change mat evokes a dream-like quality, while the brightly patterned cot/crib bumper and rug add pops of colour. A simple chest of drawers decorated with black heart-shaped stickers is straight out of *Alice In Wonderland*.

Having plenty of space inspires the children to run around and play games that take over the whole house. Although the byGraziela HQ occupies the attic, this space isn't out of bounds and the boys often sneak up to play offices while Nina is working. It's a constant juggling act, but working from home is the best solution for Nina and Simon and their three young children.

SOURCES

FASHION AND HOME STORES

Beldi Rugs
www.beldirugs.com
Handcrafted Moroccan rugs.

Bien Fait
www.bien-fait-paris.com
For exceptional wallpaper.

Blik
www.whatisblick.com
Self-adhesive wall graphics, including Dan Golden's Hole To Another Universe.

ByGraziela
www.bygraziela.com
Colourful retro fabric designs and children's products from Germany.

Corby Tindersticks
www.corbytindersticks.com
Distinctive prints, posters, cushions and height charts.

Laura Lees
www.laura-lees.com
Commission a piece of "guerilla" embroidery or attend a tuition session.

Mimi'lou
www.mimilou-shop.fr
Whimsical prints and wall stickers.

Mini Moderns
www.minimoderns.com
Fabrics, rugs and wallpapers, including designs that can be coloured in.

Nonchalant Mom
www.nonchalantmom.com
Clothes, toys and cosy homewares.

Nubie
www.nubie.co.uk
Modern nursery and children's decor.

Olive Loves Alfie
www.olivelovesalfie.co.uk
Creative family store with a carefully curated mix of art materials, children's fashion, furniture and homewares.

Rob Ryan Studio
www.robryanstudio.com
Everything from screenprints to ceramic tiles embellished with Rob's paper cuts.

Skandium
www.skandium.com
Scandinavian design store selling the bold and cheerful Marimekko fabrics.

Eva Sonaike
www.evasonaike.com
African-inspired fabrics and home decor.

Stick-Lets
www.stick-lets.com
Pocket-sized DIY kit for den-making.

The Mexican Hammock Company
www.hammocks.co.uk
Handmade hammocks as well as vibrant Mexican homewares.

BLOGS

www.ashlyngibson.co.uk
My personal blog of family life.

www.babyccinokids.com
A parenting blog by three friends in Amsterdam, London and Paris.

www.dosfamily.com
A blog about home decorating and child-friendly lifestyles by photographer Jenny Brandt.

www.ladnebebe.pl
A family style blog written by Malgosia Jakubowska in Warsaw, Poland.

www.katrinarodabaugh.com
Crafting blog by Katrina Rodabaugh, author of The Paper Playhouse.

www.lovetaza.com
A blog about Taza's adventures in New York City with her young family.

www.pirouetteblog.com
Florence Rolando's blog about family lifestyle and children's design.

www.practisingsimplicity.com
Jodi Wilson's blog celebrates family life with three children in Australia.

www.zilverblauw.nl
Anki and Casper's blog full of passion about design and family life.

SHORT FILMS

The Adventures of a Cardboard Box
https://vimeo.com/25239728
Award-winning short film that celebrates the imagination of children and the versatility of the humble cardboard box.

Caine's Arcade
www.cainesarcade.com
A short film about nine-year-old Caine's handmade cardboard arcade.

JOIN THE MOVEMENT....

Imagination Foundation
www.imagination.is
Set up to celebrate the natural creative talents of every child.

INSTAGRAM

https://instagram.com/ali__dover/
Photographer Ali Dover.

https://instagram.com/ashlyn_stylist/
A visual diary of my personal projects.

https://instagram.com/papiermache magazine
A very cute children's fashion magazine.

PICTURE CREDITS

All photography by Ben Robertson.

Endpapers The family home of Thomas, Maiken, Johanne, Selma and Kamma (designed by architects Rasmus Skaarup and Rasmus Frimer Andersen); **1** Swedish mamma of four living in Leigh-on-Sea, with Ralph; **2** The family home of Francesca Forcolini and Barry Menmuir, designers and co-founders of fashion label Labour of Love; **3** The home of photographer Emma Donnelly in Leigh-on-Sea, (www.takeapicturelady.com); **4–5** The family home of the designer Nina Nägel of byGraziela.com; **6–7** Een Schoon Oog – interior design and styling by Sonja de Groot; **8–11** 'The Wild' jungle wallpaper by Bien Fait; **8–15** The Clapton Laundry – available for photographic shoots, boutique events and creative workshops; **16** The home of photographer Emma Donnelly in Leigh-on-Sea, (www.takeapicturelady.com); **17** Chloe Thurston instagram.com/chloeuberkid, uberkid.net; **18 left** Textile designer and founder of Missemai, missemai.com; **18 right** Een Schoon Oog – interior design and styling by Sonja de Groot; **19** Textile designer and founder of Missemai www.missemai.com; **20 and 21 above left** Swedish mamma of four living in Leigh-on-Sea, with Ralph; **21 above right** The family home of Thomas, Maiken, Johanne, Selma and Kamma (designed by architects Rasmus Skaarup and Rasmus Frimer Andersen); **21 below right** The family home of the architects Jeanette and Rasmus Frisk of www.arkilab.dk; **22 left** Textile designer and founder of Missemai, missemai.com; **22 right** The family home of the designer Nina Nägel of byGraziela.com; **23–25 left** The Clapton Laundry – available for photographic shoots, boutique events and creative workshops; **25 centre** The family home of Thomas, Maiken, Johanne, Selma and Kamma (designed by architects Rasmus Skaarup and Rasmus Frimer Andersen); **25 right** Agata Hamilton www.my-home.com.pl; **26–29** The family home of the designer Nina Nägel of byGraziela.com; **30–35** The family home of Kasia Traczyk, founder of Radosna Fabryka and founder of Pacz; **36** Monika of Kaszka z Mlekiem.com, co-founder of girlsontiptoes.com; **37** The family home of Aneta of Lola y Lolo in Poland; **38 left** Textile designer and founder of Missemai, missemai.com; **38 right** The family home of the designer Nina Nägel of byGraziela.com; **39** The Clapton Laundry – available for photographic shoots, boutique events and creative workshops; **40** The family home of Thomas, Maiken, Johanne, Selma and Kamma (designed by architects Rasmus Skaarup and Rasmus Frimer Andersen); **41 above** Swedish mamma of four living in Leigh-on-Sea, with Ralph; **41 below** Chloe Thurston instagram.com/chloeuberkid, uberkid.net; **42 above** The family home of Francesca Forcolini and Barry Menmuir, designers and co-founders of fashion label Labour of Love; **42 below** The Clapton Laundry photographic location, boutique event and creative workshop; **43** The family home of the architects Jeanette and Rasmus Frisk of www.arkilab.dk; **44** The Clapton Laundry – available for photographic shoots, boutique events and creative workshops; **45** The family home of Thomas, Maiken, Johanne, Selma and Kamma (designed by architects Rasmus Skaarup and Rasmus Frimer Andersen); **46–51** Małgosia Jakubowska, ladnebebe.pl; **52** The family home of the architects Jeanette and Rasmus Frisk of www.arkilab.dk; **53** The family home of Thomas, Maiken, Johanne, Selma and Kamma (designed by architects Rasmus Skaarup and Rasmus Frimer Andersen); **54–55** The Clapton Laundry – available for photographic shoots, boutique events and creative workshops; **56–57** The family home of the designer Nina Nägel of byGraziela.com; **57 centre and right** The family home of Francesca Forcolini and Barry Menmuir, designers and co-founders of fashion label Labour of Love; **58–59** The Clapton Laundry – available for photographic shoots, boutique events and creative workshops; **60** The family home of

Thomas, Maiken, Johanne, Selma and Kamma (designed by architects Rasmus Skaarup and Rasmus Frimer Andersen); **61** The Clapton Laundry – available for photographic shoots, boutique events and creative workshops; **62 left** The family home of Francesca Forcolini and Barry Menmuir, designers and co-founders of fashion label Labour of Love; **62 centre** The family home of Thomas, Maiken, Johanne, Selma and Kamma (designed by architects Rasmus Skaarup and Rasmus Frimer Andersen); **62 right** The home of photographer Emma Donnelly in Leigh-on-Sea, (www.takeapicturelady.com); **63** The family home of Thomas, Maiken, Johanne, Selma and Kamma (designed by architects Rasmus Skaarup and Rasmus Frimer Andersen); **64** Textile designer and founder of Missemai, missemai.com; **65** The family home of Thomas, Maiken, Johanne, Selma and Kamma (designed by architects Rasmus Skaarup and Rasmus Frimer Andersen); **66–71** The family home of the architects Jeanette and Rasmus Frisk of www.arkilab.dk; **72–74** The family home of Francesca Forcolini and Barry Menmuir, designers and co-founders of fashion label Labour of Love; **75 above** Monika of Kaszka z Mlekiem.com, co-founder of girlsontiptoes.com; **75 below** Een Schoon Oog – interior design and styling by Sonja de Groot; **76–77** The family home of Thomas, Maiken, Johanne, Selma and Kamma (designed by architects Rasmus Skaarup and Rasmus Frimer Andersen); **78** The Clapton Laundry – available for photographic shoots, boutique events and creative workshops; **79** Een Schoon Oog –interior design and styling by Sonja de Groot; **80 left** Swedish mamma of four living in Leigh-on-Sea, with Ralph; **80 right** Een Schoon Oog – interior design and styling by Sonja de Groot; **81** The family home of Ewa Solarz in Poland; **82** Agata Hamilton www.my-home.com.pl; **83** The Clapton Laundry – available for photographic shoots, boutique events and creative workshops; **84–91** The family home of Francesca Forcolini and Barry Menmuir, designers and co-founders of fashion label Labour of Love; **92** Agata Hamilton www.my-home.com.pl; **93** Chloe Thurston instagram.com/chloeuberkid, uberkid.net; **94 left** Een Schoon Oog – interior design and styling by Sonja de Groot; **94 right** The family home of Thomas, Maiken, Johanne, Selma and Kamma (designed by architects Rasmus Skaarup and Rasmus Frimer Andersen); **95** The family home of Kasia Traczyk, founder of Radosna Fabryka and founder of Pacz; **96 and 97 left** The family home of Francesca Forcolini and Barry Menmuir, designers and co-founders of fashion label Labour of Love; **97 above right** Chloe Thurston instagram.com/chloeuberkid, uberkid.net; **97 below right** The Clapton Laundry – available for photographic shoots, boutique events and creative workshops; **98 left** Een Schoon Oog – interior design and styling by Sonja de Groot; **98 right and 99** The Clapton Laundry – available for photographic shoots, boutique events and creative workshops; **100** Agata Hamilton www.my-home.com.pl; **101 left** The house of Silvia and Bart Pogoda in Poland; **101 right** Monika of Kaszka z Mlekiem.com, co-founder of girlsontiptoes.com; **102** The Clapton Laundry – available for photographic shoots, boutique events and creative workshops; **103** The home of photographer Emma Donnelly in Leigh-on-Sea, (www.takeapicturelady.com); **104–111** Agata Hamilton www.my-home.com.pl; **112–113** Chloe Thurston instagram.com/chloeuberkid, uberkid.net; **114 and 115 left** The family home of Francesca Forcolini and Barry Menmuir, designers and co-founders of fashion label Labour of Love; **115 right** Monika of Kaszka z Mlekiem.com, co-founder of girlsontiptoes.com; **116–117** The Clapton Laundry – available for photographic shoots, boutique events and creative workshops; **118** Een Schoon Oog – interior design and styling by Sonja de Groot; **119 above** Monika of Kaszka z Mlekiem.com, co-founder of girlsontiptoes.com; **119 below** The family home of Ewa Solarz in Poland; **120** The family home of Aneta of Lola y Lolo in Poland; **121** The family home of the designer Nina Nägel of byGraziela.com; **122–123** The family

home of Ewa Solarz in Poland; **124–129** Chloe Thurston instagram.com/chloeuberkid, uberkid.net; **130–131** The family home of the designer Nina Nägel of byGraziela.com; **132 left** The house of Silvia and Bart Pogoda in Poland; **132 right** Monika of Kaszka z Mlekiem.com, co-founder of girlsontiptoes.com; **133** Agata Hamilton www.my-home.com.pl; **134–135** Chloe Thurston instagram.com/chloeuberkid, uberkid.net; **136 left** Chloe Thurston instagram.com/chloeuberkid, uberkid.net; **136 above right** The family home of Thomas, Maiken, Johanne, Selma and Kamma (designed by architects Rasmus Skaarup and Rasmus Frimer Andersen); **136 below right** Monika of Kaszka z Mlekiem.com, co-founder of girlsontiptoes.com; **137** Chloe Thurston instagram.com/chloeuberkid, uberkid.net; **138–139 left** The home of photographer Emma Donnelly in Leigh-on-Sea, (www.takeapicturelady.com); **139 right** Agata Hamilton www.my-home.com.pl; **140** The family home of Thomas, Maiken, Johanne, Selma and Kamma (designed by architects Rasmus Skaarup and Rasmus Frimer Andersen); **141** Een Schoon Oog – interior design and styling by Sonja de Groot; **142–143 above** The home of photographer Emma Donnelly in Leigh-on-Sea, (www.takeapicturelady.com); **143 below right, 144 and 145 below** The family home of Aneta of Lola y Lolo in Poland; **145 above** The Clapton Laundry – available for photographic shoots, boutique events and creative workshops; **146–156** The family home of the designer Nina Nägel of byGraziela.com; **157** The family home of Francesca Forcolini and Barry Menmuir, designers and co-founders of fashion label Labour of Love; **160** Chloe Thurston instagram.com/chloeuberkid, uberkid.net.

BUSINESS CREDITS

**Rasmus Frimer Andersen
and Rasmus Skaarup**
Architects
2r arkitekter ApS
Trepkasgade 9
2100 Copenhagen
Denmark
T: +45 40 34 16 42
E: rs@a2rk.dk
www.2r-arkitekter.dk
*Pages 21 above right, 25 centre, 40,
45, 53, 60, 62 centre, 63, 65, 76–77,
94 right, 136 above right, 140.*

**Ark_lab
Democratic Urban Design and
Strategy**
Birkegade 4
2200 Copenhagen
Denmark
E: mail@arkilab.dk
www.arkilab.dk
Pages 21 below right, 43, 52, 66–71.

The Clapton Laundry
Photographic Location
E: hello@ashlyngibson.co.uk
*Pages 8–15, 23, 24, 25 left, 39, 42
below, 44, 54–55, 58–59, 61, 78, 83,
97 below right, 98 right, 99, 102,
116–117, 145 above.*

Emma Donnelly
Photographer
www.takeapicturelady.com
*Pages 3, 16, 62 right, 103, 138,
139 left, 142, 143 above.*

**Sonja de Groot
Een Schoon Oog**
Interior Styling
T: + 31 6 10 35 01 00
E: Sonja@eenschoonoog.nl
www.eenschoonoog.nl
*Pages 6–7, 18 right, 75 below, 79,
80 right, 94 left, 98 left, 118, 141.*

**Agata Hamilton
My Home**
Furniture, Lighting and Interiors
www.my-home.com.pl
*Pages 25 right, 82, 92, 100, 104–111,
133, 139 right.*

Kaszka z Mlekiem
www.kaszkazmlekiem.wordpress.com
*Pages 36, 75 above, 101 right, 115
right, 119 above left, 132 right, 136
below right.*

Małgosia Jakubowska
ladnebebe.pl
Pages 46–51.

Labour of Love
www.labour-of-love.co.uk
E: info@labour-of-love.co.uk
*2, 42 above, 57 centre, 57 right, 62
left, 72–74, 84–91, 96, 97 left, 114,
115 left, 157.*

Lola y Lolo
Bedding and accessories
www.lolaylolo.com
*Pages 37, 120, 143 below right, 144,
145 below.*

Missemai
Prints and junior bed linen
missemai.com
Pages 18 left, 19, 22 left, 38 left, 64.

**Nina Nägel
byGraziela**
Original designs by Graziela Preiser
www.bygraziela.com
*Pages 4–5, 22 right, 26–29, 38 right,
56–57, 121, 130–11, 146–156.*

OtherLetters
Bringing words and parties to life
www.otherletters.co.uk
*Pages 1, 20, 21 above left, 41 above,
80 left.*

Radosna Fabryka
www.radosnafabryka.pl
Pages 30–35, 95.

Silvia Pogoda
Photographer
www.silviapogoda.com
and
www.iwanttobeafool.com
Pages 101 left, 132 left.

Ewa Solarz
E: ewa.solarz@domplusdom.pl
www.domplusdom.pl
Pages 81, 119 below, 122–123.

Chloe Thurston
instagram.com/chloeuberkid
uberkid.net
*Pages 17, 41 below, 93, 97 above
right, 112–113, 124–129, 134–135,
136 left, 137, 160.*

INDEX

ACKNOWLEDGMENTS

A book about family style is only as inspiring as the people in it. I feel very lucky to have discovered so many unique and creative families. A huge thank you to photographer Ben Robertson, and to my wonderful team at Ryland Peters and Small, for championing my second book and sharing my vision.

While I have been working on my book, a wonderful team of people have supported me and kept my world turning. Thank you to Alison and Donna for keeping the doors open at Olive Loves Alfie. To Olive, my supremely cool 12 year old, who understands the importance of following your dreams. To Matthew for the love he gives to me and everything that I do. And finally to my mum who continues to inspire me with her love, creativity and generosity.